Hermeneutical Agnosticism
A Critique of Subjectivism in Biblical Interpretation

Jody L. Apple

Foreword by
Thomas B. Warren, Ph.D.

New Testament Christian Press/Media, PA 19063

HERMENEUTICAL AGNOSTICISM: A Critique of Subjectivism in Biblical Interpretation

copyright © 1985 by Jody L. Apple

All rights reserved worldwide. No part of this work may be reproduced, stored in a retrieval system, or transmitted by any means, electronic, mechanical, magnetic, chemical, optical, manual, or otherwise, including photocopying, without the written permission of the publisher, except as necessary for purposes of reviewing and or quoting the work, in which case copies of such should be sent to the publisher.

Published by **NEW TESTAMENT CHRISTIAN PRESS**
P.O. Box 1694
Media, PA. 19063

Library of Congress Catalog Card Number: 84-62067

ISBN 0-931247-00-4

To my precious wife Evelyn

TABLE OF CONTENTS

	TABLE OF CONTENTS........................	i
	FOREWORD.................................	iv
	REVIEW OF HERMENEUTICAL AGNOSTICISM......	vii
	AUTHOR'S PREFACE.........................	ix
I:	INTRODUCTION.............................	1
II:	THE PROBLEM AND ITS IMPORTANCE...........	3
III:	TOWARD A SOLUTION........................	7
IV:	THE THESIS...............................	8
	The Thesis Explained.....................	9
	The Meaning Of Premise Four..............	14
V:	GENERAL DEFINITIONS......................	19
	God......................................	19
	The Bible................................	20
	Revelation...............................	21
	Inspiration..............................	21
	Agnosticism..............................	22
	Communication............................	24
	Hermeneutics.............................	25
	Logic....................................	27
	The Laws Of Thought......................	28
	The Law Of Rationality...................	28
	Epistemology.............................	29
VI:	PRESUPPOSITIONS..........................	36
VII:	LIMITATIONS..............................	38
VIII:	EXAMPLES OF THE PROBLEM..................	41
	Example One..............................	42

Example Two..............................	45
Example Three............................	55
Conclusion...............................	58

IX-A: ARGUMENTATION AGAINST AGNOSTICISM....... 63
    The Necessity Of Hermeneutics........... 63
    General Arguments....................... 72
    Argument #1............................. 76
    Argument #2............................. 76
    Argument #3............................. 78

IX-B: ARGUMENTATION AGAINST AGNOSTICISM....... 83
    Specific Arguments...................... 83
    Argument #1............................. 84
    Argument #2............................. 86
    Argument #3............................. 89

IX-C: ARGUMENTATION AGAINST AGNOSTICISM....... 102
    Argument #4............................. 102

X: ARGUMENTATION IN DEFENSE OF THESIS...... 109
    Positive Argumentation.................. 110
    Argument #1............................. 119
    Argument #2............................. 120
    Argument #1-A........................... 121
    Argument #3............................. 123
    Argument #3-A........................... 125
    Argument #4............................. 128

XI: OBJECTIONS TO THE THESIS CONSIDERED..... 134
    Objection #1............................ 134
    Objection #2............................ 140
    Objection #3............................ 140
    Objection #4............................ 148
    Objection #5............................ 148
    Objection #6............................ 151

XII: PRACTICAL APPLICATIONS................... 154
    God Demands That Truth Be Taught........ 154
    God Demands That Error Be Refuted....... 155

    Truth and Error Are Distinguishable..... 157
    God Expects Obedience To Truth.......... 159
    Summary................................. 161

XIII:CONCLUSION............................. 163

    SELECTED BIBLIOGRAPHY................... 165

    INDEX................................... 170

FOREWORD

One of the greatest pleasures of a teacher is surely that of seeing those whom he has taught become outstanding teachers and/or writers. Thus, since the writer of this book (which, with slight modifications, was his thesis for the Master of Arts degree) is a former student of mine and, further, since the man who was his counselor for that writing (Professor Mac Deaver) is also a former student of mine (and who wrote—under my direct supervision—a thesis on much the same subject), it gives me an unusual amount of pleasure to be privileged to write a few words which will serve as the Foreword to this book.

In this book, Jody Apple deals with one of the most crucial of all topics, especially at this time: **hermeneutical agnosticism.** This is the case, because to be an "agnostic" (at least in the usual sense in which that word is used in regard to religious or theological matters) is to claim to <u>know</u> that <u>no</u> <u>one</u> can know that such propositions as: "God does exist," "The Bible is the word of God," "Jesus Christ is the Son of God," "The Bible teaches that, to be saved from sins, one must be baptized in the name of Christ" are true.

The importance of espousing and asserting such an error (agnosticism) is seen in the fact that it implies that, for all any one knows, God does not exist. Further, it is obvious that if God does not exist, then the Bible <u>cannot</u> be the word of God. Still further, if the Bible <u>is not</u> the word of God, then it should be rejected by all men. Thus, if men cannot <u>know</u> both that God does exist and that the Bible is His word, then the implications are serious indeed.

Further, even if one were to grant (in contradiction to the philosophical doctrine of agnosticism) that it is at least possible for one to come to <u>know</u> that God <u>does</u> exist and that the Bible is the word of God, such admission would, in the "long run," be fruitless if he still maintained that no one can really come to <u>know</u> what the Bible teaches about what men must <u>do</u> to <u>become</u> saved and to <u>remain</u> saved. The Bible would be useless if it is simply <u>not possible</u> for any one to learn (come to know) what it teaches.

Apple deals with these crucial matters and shows the absurdity of thoroughgoing agnosticism. Thoroughgoing agnosticism is obviously self-contradictory. The basic affirmation of agnosticism is: "I know that no one knows anything." Since this affirmation is obviously false (since it is self-contradictory), it follows that the doctrine of agnosticism is false.

The Bible plainly teaches that men <u>can know</u> that God does exist (cf. Psalm 19:1; Romans 1:18-25; John 17:3; Acts 17:22-31; et al.), that men <u>can know</u> that the Bible is the word of God (see details in <u>The Case For Christianity</u> by Thomas B. Warren), that men <u>can know</u> that Jesus Christ is the Son of God (cf. Acts 2:22-36; John 20:30-31). Men can also know that no man can be saved without faith (Hebrews 11:6; John 8:24; 20:30-31; Mark 16:15-16; et al.). Yet, <u>knowledge</u> of the truth must precede Biblical faith (Romans 10:17; Acts 2:22-36). One comes to know the truth (John 8:32) and is made free (from his sins) when he truly trusts in God by obeying His word (cf. Proverbs 3:5-6; Romans 4:20-21; Hebrews 5:8-9). To act by faith is to act by taking God at his word—being persuaded that God will do exactly as He says (in His word) that He will do (Romans 4:20-21). God does not lie; He always tells the truth (Hebrews 6:18; Titus 1:2; I Samuel 15:29; et al.).

The basic argument in regard to hermeneutical knowledge (which, incidentally, I devised many years ago and have taught to many students both on the undergraduate and graduate levels since no later than 1964) involves these propositions: (1) men can know that God exists, (2) men can know that the Bible is the word of God, (3) men can know that the Bible teaches that Jesus Christ is the Son of God and that, to be saved, men must believe in, love and obey Him, being baptized by His authority to obtain the remission of sins by being baptized <u>unto</u> the remission of sins and then, as a child of God, to live a faithful life of "walking in the light" of God's word (I John 1:7; Revelation 2:10).

It is clear that men can <u>know</u> how to arrive at the truth of what the Bible tea<u>ches.</u> (I have explained the basic "how" of this in two books: (1) <u>Logic and the Bible</u> and <u>When Is An "Example" Binding?</u> as well as in a number of journal articles.)

It is indeed a source of pleasure to me to see the production of this present book—written by one of my former students, Jody Apple, and overseen (as faculty advisor) by another student of mine, Mac Deaver.

It is my sincere wish that every former student of mine would do such good works as Apple has done in writing this present book. It is my hope and sincere desire, coupled with expectation, that many more books will come from the pen of Jody Apple. May God bless him to that end is my prayer.

Thomas B. Warren, Ph.D
December 8, 1984

A REVIEW OF HERMENEUTICAL AGNOSTICISM

There is no greater heresy presently troubling the church than that of agnosticism. And, to the extent that the church becomes agnostic, she is to that extent apostate.

Brother Jody Apple has rendered the church a tremendous service in his work <u>Hermeneutical Agnosticism</u>, a book which deserves a wide circulation and concentrated study on the part of those who would know better how to defend the "knowability" of saving truth.

In our day more and more people (including some brethren) are taking the position that one cannot really be sure of any truth. The notion that one cannot make absolute knowledge claims is permeating the minds of far too many brethren.

While brethren of the agnostic bent still want to "hold on" to God's existence...they deny that God has communicated to man in such a way that a man can really know beyond the shadow of a doubt what he must do to be saved.

The Bible, of course, answers such nonsense. And in <u>Hermeneutical Agnosticism</u>, brother Apple has taken the biblical position that man can know saving truth...and has proven the case.

He has demonstrated with logical precision the verification of the possibility of knowledge, and he has with equal precision shown the fallaciousness involved in the attempt to deny that one can really come down conclusively on the absolutely knowing side of saving truth.

With symbolic logic brother Apple neatly wraps up his position. The symbols employed will be appreciated by the more advanced student, and the explanation of them prevents the discussion of this vital material from going beyond the capability of those readers not familiar with a symbolic logic presentation.

<u>Hermeneutical Agnosticism</u> is a tremendous book

dealing with such a fundamental and extremely important issue. The truth regarding the possibility of knowing is set out in its strength, and the view that one cannot know what the Bible teaches regarding salvation is exposed for what it is in all its weakness.

The situation demands that faithful brethren know what the agnostics among us are doing to us. Every faithful Christian would do himself an immeasurable service in digesting the material contained in <u>Hermeneutical Agnosticism</u>. He would be far better prepared to answer the agnostic declarations that are being made more and more among, and by, God's people.

Mac Deaver
September 17, 1984

AUTHOR'S PREFACE AND ACKNOWLEDGEMENTS

The concept of this book originated a few short years ago as I encountered what seemed to be an unusual number of articles and speeches that espoused a peculiar agnostic stance. I say "peculiar" for I believe this form of agnosticism differs from the general philosophical and theological agnosticism promoted almost everywhere.

This brand of agnosticism, dubbed "hermeneutical agnosticism" by this writer, is much more subtle, and therefore harder to detect than the average "run-of-the-mill" philosophical and theological agnosticism. It is "hermeneutical" in that it is directly related to one's view of Biblical interpretation. The principle concept of this idea is one which raises suspicions with regard to absolute and objective interpretations of the scriptures. Given hermeneutical agnosticism in its extreme form, it would be impossible to say with certainty that man can know any Bible truth.

Hermeneutical agnosticism can appear in a number of ways. In general form it is seen in the oft repeated phrase: "You can get whatever you want to out of the Bible." It also appears in specific form with regard to specific situations: "I don't believe we can know what God wanted man to do concerning baptism, marriage, divorce and remarriage, et al."

To be sure, there are elements of Bible teaching about which we can rightly claim to say "I don't know," but the application of this claim to areas that are essential for one's salvation can be, and is, dangerous. This is where "hermeneutical agnosticism" seems to be the strongest. On those issues where we fear to make a decision we are most prone to claim "No one can know." We may say that because we really believe it cannot be known by man, or simply because we do not know it. We must remember, however, that our lack of knowledge and conviction about a given Bible subject does not preclude the same on the part of others.

The occurrence of hermeneutical agnosticism is widespread. It can, and does, affect just about every Bible truth one can imagine. The examples cited in chapter eight are but a sampling of those that could be offered, and they, rather than others, are given only because I discovered them all at about the same time, and because of the inter-relationships they seem to have with each other. They were not singled out for any other reasons.

With regard to the development of this work, I would be most unkind if I did not mention some of those who worked with me. Though the actual form and content of this work is solely the responsibility of the writer, it could not have been completed without the assistance of many faithful friends.

Mac Deaver, my supervisor for this guided research thesis at Tennessee Bible College, has been a tremendous help from start to finish. He carefully read and critiqued this work in its various stages from the start, and kindly agreed to re-read it as it was being rewritten for publication. I appreciate his help very much.

Thomas B. Warren, who penned the foreword for the book, has also been a great help. I am thankful that I was blessed with the opportunity to study under him at the graduate school. His dedication to upholding the truth and defending it against every false way is admired by many...myself included. I hope and pray that the Lord will continue to bless him in his continued efforts at writing and lecturing on apologetic related themes.

I am also thankful to the administration, faculty, staff, and students of **Tennessee Bible College**, especially the **Graduate School of Christian Doctrine and Apologetics,** who worked and studied at the school between 1979 and 1982. I have many fond memories of these years.

The bulk of this material was written while I worked with the **Rome church of Christ** near Lebanon,

Tennessee. I am thankful to the good brethren at Rome for their loving kindness expressed to me and my family while we labored with them for three years.

This book was completely rewritten and edited while laboring with the **Springfield church of Christ** near Philadelphia. I am thankful for the opportunity to work with this new church as we seek to spread the gospel of Christ in this great urban area.

The elders of the **Needmore church of Christ, (Raymond Burkhart, Travis Smith, and Marshall Burkhart)** along with the minister of the Needmore church **(Tony Lawrence)** are also to be thanked. They, along with the great Needmore congregation and other individuals and churches, are directly responsible for my presence in the Philadelphia area. A church stronger than the Needmore church would be hard to find!

Last, but certainly not least, I am thankful to many close friends and beloved family members. The numerous discussions that I have had with men that love the truth have had an impact, not only upon this book, but upon my life as well. I have a special affection for those men who put away the secular pursuits of life and seek to stand firmly upon the Bible and preach its beautiful truths for the world to hear. There can be no nobler profession than preaching the gospel...and to all those faithful gospel preachers that I have met, talked with, and read about...I thank you greatly!

My family has been a great help to me in so many ways. My precious wife Evelyn has been a source of constant strength to me for many years, and I hope, for many more to come. I doubt very seriously if a more intelligent, witty, warm, and loving, Christian wife and mother exists anywhere. She has stood beside me in every good work that I have set in mind to do, and I am confident that she will ever do so.

My two sons, Jonathan and Benjamin, are also to be thanked. They patiently endured as "Daddy" spent many long hours in front of his computer diligently typing and retyping the final manuscript. It is my hope and prayer that these two wonderful boys will grow to be strong and faithful Christian gentlemen.

It has been the aim of this writer throughout this work to set forth, strongly and clearly, a very important and fundamental principle taught within the pages of God's word. Every responsible person has the ability to read and understand the teachings of God's word for himself, and to act upon those teachings in such a way as to be pleasing to his Creator and Lord. It is my sincere and fervent prayer that you, the reader, will gain a greater appreciation for this sublime truth.

Jody L. Apple
December 27, 1984

HERMENEUTICAL AGNOSTICISM

CHAPTER ONE: INTRODUCTION

Agnosticism, that particular tenet of belief usually taken to be the half-way point between theism and atheism, has plagued Biblical theism in numerous fashions. Indeed, as it originated by T.H. Huxley, the term had exclusive reference to the question of God's existence.[1] Relative to that question, agnosticism quite simply claims that there is insufficient evidence to warrant any conclusion, either positively or negatively, that such a being as God exists.

But agnosticism has other areas of influence. In addition to casting doubts relative to the instantiation of maximal greatness (i.e., the existence of God), agnosticism is also seen manifested in the sphere of the communicative ability of God.[2] Is the Bible the real and actual word of God, or is it just another work of man? If it is the word of God, can it be understood by man today?

These two questions involve the subjects of the inspiration, the authority, and the interpretation of the Bible. With regard to these areas, the scepticism promoted by agnosticism has also cast its doubts. According to agnosticism, therefore, one can be no more sure of the credibility and/or the interpretation of the Bible, than he can be of the existence of God. All of these areas of theism are open to question and criticism.

The basic argument for Christianity, as it is set forth by Dr. Thomas B. Warren, involves an argument which includes all three of these important elements.[3]

That argument, which shall be discussed in more detail later, basically states that: (1) if we can know that God exists, and (2) if we can know that the Bible is the word of God, and (3) if we can know that the Bible teaches X, where X is any true Bible proposition, then (4) we can know the truth of proposition X.

It is evident, therefore, that the subject of agnosticism is important as it relates to this basic argument, for it levels its suspicions at each of the three conjuncts forming the antecedent of the basic argument for Christianity.

This work will, however, only be devoted to a study of the third area, the realm of Biblical interpretation, commonly styled hermeneutics. Though this facet will be the focus of this endeavor, due to its inextricable relationship to the other two tenets of Biblical theism (i.e., the existence of God and the inspiration/authority of the Bible), it (i.e., hermeneutics) must of necessity be studied in light of these other elements of theism.

---

1. Kai Nielsen, "Agnosticism" in <u>Dictionary of the History of Ideas</u> (New York: Charles Scribner's Sons, Publishers, 1973), Vol. 1, p.17

2. This assumes, of course, that God does exist.

3. For this information I am indebted to Dr. Thomas B. Warren's class "Critique of Atheism," Tennessee Graduate School of Christian Doctrine and Apologetics, Fall 1979.

CHAPTER TWO: THE PROBLEM OF AGNOSTICISM

Agnosticism, as it is applied to the realm of Biblical hermeneutics, causes an almost unlimited number of problems for theism. If agnosticism is correct in asserting that man can not know the meaning and intent of the Bible, then theism as we know it is meaningless.[1]

In its espousal of a faulty hermeneutical method, and even the possibility of no method of understanding the Bible, agnosticism produces and encourages the following results: (1) It produces a world replete with different religious beliefs and different religious teachings. (2) It results in numerous different explanations (i.e., interpretations) of the Bible. (3) It aids in the proliferation of a multiplicity of different religious organizations. (4) It encourages the teaching of error. (5) It increases the probability of believing in error as if it were truth.

(6) It increases the probability that more people will believe error, teach it, and be lost as a result of it. (7) Due to its promotion of different interpretations of the Bible and the uncertainty of all of them, agnosticism encourages the world to disbelieve in the Bible as the word of God, and in the objective truths found within it. (8) Through agnosticism in Biblical interpretation, many will be caused to remain in unbelief. (9) Through differences in interpretation, agnosticism will cause some to deny that there is a God which could give any revelation to mankind. (10) These differences in interpretation will cause many to turn to the philosophies of men. (11) Numerous interpretations of the Bible will cause either ill feelings, or a general attitude of indifference to the religious world at large. And, (12) agnosticism and its resultant divergent interpretations will cause many to deny many basic Bible truths, such as the existence of the one true church of Christ, the necessity of baptism for the remission of sins, and many other essential

tenets of New Testament Christianity.

Furthermore, agnosticism, as it encourages numerous opposing interpretations (or no interpretation at all), will be responsible for intensified differences within the world of religion itself. False interpretations will continue to multiply as different religious organizations will: (1) use their own interpretations to **'prove'** their respective doctrines, (2) use their interpretations to keep the Bible a **'mystery'**, and (3) use their interpretations to **'disprove'** the credibility and the teachings of other religious groups which interpret the Bible in a way foreign to themselves.

The problem of hermeneutical agnosticism is further evidenced by its implications concerning the nature and the existence of God, and the nature of God's revelation, the Bible (if indeed God has revealed himself through the Bible). If, as per agnosticism, we can not be absolutely sure with respect to any interpretation of a Bible passage, then we can not be sure that anything we teach or believe is actually the truth. Robert Flint says that such thinking "so exaggerated the relativity alike of sense and of thought as to leave no room for a reasonable trust in the certainty of any kind of knowledge."[2]

If such is true, then we can not know numerous beliefs commonly advocated by the religious world to be true. We could not know: (1) that Jesus was the Son of God, (2) that Jesus was conceived of a virgin, (3) the certainty of the resurrection of Jesus, (4) what we must do or know in order to be found in favor with God, (5) that man is an immortal being made in the image of God, (6) the true origin of the universe and the true purpose of man, and (7) any other doctrine which had the Bible as its basis for belief.

More specifically, with regard to the existence of God (if there is a God), agnosticism informs us, through its implications, that God cannot communicate to man through a written revelation in such a way as to be understood by mankind. Should this be true, it implies serious consequences respecting the nature of God.

If the Bible were, in reality, the revelation of God, yet at the same time incapable of being properly understood as God intended, then such a position would indicate the following possibilities: (1) God may not be **powerful** enough to communicate to mankind through the means of written revelation. (2) God may not be **wise** enough to communicate to man in this fashion. Or, (3) God may not have the **desire** to communicate to mankind through this method.

Should agnosticism grant that the Bible is the word of God, and that it is subject to understanding, but that no one could, in actuality, understand it, then God has provided us with a totally useless revelation. In fact, if this were the case, **the Bible would not even be considered as revelation.** This latter situation also implies a lack of **wisdom** on the part of God.

If any of these above positions is true, then either the omnipotence, the omniscience, or the omnibenevolence of God is less than infinite. If this be true, then God, as the Bible speaks of God, does not exist, and the "existence" of a finite "God" equals the non-existence of any God.

Finally, if the position of hermeneutical agnosticism is adhered to fully, one will be in the possible position of denying that certain propositions can be known, which in reality are subject to cognition. This posture, therefore, severely limits its approach to Biblical understanding, or any other Bible related discipline (e.g., apologetics, etc.).

For example, if proposition X is true, and if proposition X is subject to human cognition, and if proposition X is **necessary** to sustain doctrine Y, then it will be **impossible** to prove doctrine Y should one hold to the position that proposition X **was not** subject to human knowledge. If doctrine Y were an integral element of that person's theology, his "plan of salvation" for instance, then it would be **impossible** for a proponent of such a religious belief to have due reason for believing his position. All of this resulted from the basic premise of denying the ability to know the truth of proposition X, where proposition X represents a true Bible proposition which in reality is subject to cognition.

On the other hand, should the Bible be subject to human understanding, a person who believed in a specific "plan of salvation," of which doctrine Y was an integral element, could know his doctrine to be true if he knew that proposition X were true, and that proposition X was subject to cognition, and that proposition X implied the truthfulness of doctrine Y.

The difference, therefore, between hermeneutical agnosticism and Biblical theism, boils down to **not-knowing versus knowing**, as it relates to the truthfulness of the propositions of Scripture.

---

1. See J.S. Lamar's discussion of the implications of such scepticism in J.S. Lamar, Organon Of Scripture (Philadelphia: J.B. Lippincott and Co., 1860, reprinted by The Old Paths Book Club, 1952), p. 20ff

2. Robert Flint, Agnosticism (New York: Charles Scribner's Sons, 1903), p. 92

CHAPTER THREE: TOWARD A SOLUTION

Having completed the general introduction and the statement of the problem, it becomes necessary to mention the direction of the remainder of this book.

The simplest approach, I suppose, would involve a listing of the weaknesses of agnosticism in Biblical interpretation, along with appropriate critical comments. Such an approach, however, assumes too much.

It is important that the reader understand the foundations upon which the writer makes his arguments and draws his conclusions. For that reason, it is imperative that numerous fundamental premises be set forth. Then, having fully understood the groundwork of the issue, the reader will be in a much better position to comprehend the writer's reasoned arguments and conclusions.

Immediately following this section, therefore, the following subjects will be presented in the following order: (1) The specific thesis of the paper will be presented and discussed. (2) Definitions crucial to this book will be explained. (3) The presuppositions (assumptions) that the author makes will be detailed. (4) The limitations of this book will be outlined. (5) Some specific examples of the problem of hermeneutical agnosticism will be presented. (6) Argumentation against hermeneutical agnosticism will be set forth. (7) Argumentation in defense of the thesis of this book will be discussed. (8) Possible objections to the book's thesis will be considered. (9) Some practical applications of the thesis will be examined. And, (10) some concluding and summary remarks will close out our study.

CHAPTER FOUR: THE THESIS

Most of the written works devoted to a discussion of the subject of Biblical interpretation concern themselves with a listing, exposition, and explanation of certain rules and methods of hermeneutics. Though this information and style of approach is important, very few deal with the fundamental question in hermeneutics: **CAN WE KNOW THAT THE BIBLE TEACHES DOCTRINE X, WHERE X REPRESENTS ANY TRUE BIBLE PROPOSITION?** Most works simply assume that such is possible, and though this is a correct assumption (as will be demonstrated by this work), they never set forth the case to **prove**, in a demonstrative way, that this assumption is correct.

It is the purpose of this book, therefore, not to deal exclusively with methods and principles of interpretation, but rather to deal with the more fundamental question: can we **KNOW** (i.e., understand) the Bible?

Other related questions are: To what extent can we understand the Bible? What can we not understand (if anything) about the Bible? **Why can we not understand certain things about the Bible?** What are the limits of Bible knowledge? It is the basic thesis of this work to show that we can **KNOW**, as the Bible teaches we can know, **ALL** that is **NECESSARY** for the **SALVATION** of our souls.

In opposition to this thesis, agnosticism as it relates to Biblical interpretation, or hermeneutical agnosticism, advocates that the Bible cannot be sufficiently understood in numerous areas, one of which directly involves the subject of soteriology (salvation). In this regard, some "conservative evangelicals," such as Clark Pinnock, err when they, in an effort to defend objectivism, say such things as "The task is never done, for God always has yet more light and truth to give from His Holy Word. Our hermeneutic is never exhaustive and never infallible."[1]

Though we may ever continue to learn new things about some specific Bible passage, this is not to say that the acquisition of new knowledge automatically demands the falsification of "old" knowledge. If a proposition is true, it remains true, regardless of the number of additional and related propositions we learn to be true. It is correct, then, in light of the ongoing discoveries in the field of archaeology, for example, to state that we can always learn more about the Bible...**but it is incorrect to affirm that what has been known, or what is presently known, is fallible.**

The Thesis Explained

With regard to the importance and purpose of Bible study, Roy Deaver has noted the following:

> We must study the Bible with proper regard for its <u>purpose</u>. The Bible relates to the <u>need</u> for human redemption. This is the fundamental thought dealt with in the first three chapters of Genesis: God sets before us the explanation as to where there was (and is) a need for the plan of redemption. The Bible teaches that <u>all</u> accountable persons share in this need, Romans 3:22, 23; 1 John 1:8-10. The Bible shows that redemption is <u>through Jesus Christ</u>, Romans 3:24; Ephesians 1:7; Colossians 1:14; Galatians 1:4. The Old Testament message points the way to Christ and prepares for Him and His message. This is the testimony of dozens of passages, such as Luke 24:13-25; John 5:39, 46; 1 Peter 1:10-12. The sacred plan for human redemption brings honor and <u>glory to God</u>. This fact is mentioned in Ephesians 1:6; 3:21; Romans 16:27; Galatians 1:5; Philippians 2:11; Romans

11:36. Consideration of these fundamental facts makes obvious the purpose of the Bible: THE GLORY OF GOD, AND THE SALVATION OF MAN, THROUGH JESUS CHRIST OUR LORD. This is the basic point in Bible study. This is the divine purpose line which runs from the first verse of Genesis through the last verse of the Revelation.[2]

The Bible, therefore, must be studied according to its purpose, but we must note that the purpose of the Bible is directly related to the purpose, or the mission, of God the Father, God the Son, and the church, each of which will be briefly discussed here.

First, It is God's purpose and desire to provide for the salvation of the souls of mankind. God does not want any person to perish (II Peter 3:9). He wants all men to repent (Acts 17:30). God wants all to come to salvation (I Timothy 2:3-4), and he has provided the means whereby man might come to that salvation (Titus 2:11ff). That means involved the life and the death of God's only begotten son, Jesus the Christ.

Second, Christ, being the "express image" of his Father (Hebrews 1:3), has the same will, goal, and purpose as does the Father. This should come as no surprise, for Jesus often mentioned during his life the singularity of purpose that existed between the Father and the Son (John 4:34; Matthew 19:11; Luke 19:10; et. al.). Thus, Christ, according to his own will and the will of God, came to offer his life for the salvation of all mankind (II Corinthians 5:21).

Third, during his earthly ministry, Jesus made frequent mention of the church, the kingdom of God (Matthew 4:17; 16:18; Mark 9:1; et. al.). This kingdom, or church (Matthew 16:18-19), was to be established by Christ following his death, burial, resurrection, and ascension (Luke 24:44ff; Matthew 28:18ff; Acts 1:1-8; 2:1-47). According to the prophets, this institution came to fruition on the day of

Pentecost following the ascension of Christ (Isaiah 2:1-4; Micah 4:1-2; Daniel 2:44; Joel 2:28-32; Acts 2:1-47).

The church was not a substitution for any earthly kingdom that Christ failed to establish, but was, and is, part of the eternal plan of God for the redemption of mankind (Ephesians 3:8-11). Just as Christ's will and purpose was identical with the will of his Father, so is the will, or purpose, of the church identical with the will of Christ. Ephesians 3:10-11, noted above, informs us that the eternal purpose of the church was to make known God's will. This passage does not mean that the truth of the mystery of God is to be known only by those who are Christians, but it does mean that the church is to be involved in the process by which others learn of the truth. First and foremost, the very existence of the church of Christ is a manifestation of the wisdom of God. Weymouth's translation, <u>The New Testament In Modern Speech</u>, renders this section of the passage "that the Church might now be used to display...the innumerable aspects of God's wisdom."

Second, the church makes known the wisdom of God by proclaiming God's holy and revealed word. It is through the teaching and preaching of the gospel that the church which Jesus established is involved in the mission and work of God the Father and God the Son. That the church is to be involved in this mission is evidenced by a study of the book of Acts.

Jesus, immediately prior to his ascension, told his disciples that they "shall be witnesses unto me both in Jerusalem, and in all Judea, and in Samaria, and unto the uttermost part of the earth" (Acts 1:8). This four-fold division forms the basic outline of evangelism that is represented throughout the remainder of the book. The church, beginning at Jerusalem, proclaimed the gospel of Christ. As the church grew in number and in strength, so the reaches of its influence grew. Acts 8 portrays the preaching of the gospel in Samaria by Philip. Acts 9 depicts the conversion of Saul of Tarsus, who was to become a great missionary to the Gentile world. Acts 10 informs us of the conversion of the household of Cornelius, the Gentile centurion. The remainder of the book of Acts continues this trend toward the evangelization of the entire world. Several years latter, as Paul wrote to the Christians in Colossae, he indicated that the gospel had gone into "all the world" and "was preached to every creature which is under heaven" (Colossians 1:6, 23).

Finally, closely related to the importance of the church's role in the plan of God, is the role played by the word of God. As Christians traveled the lands of the New Testament world they took with them and proclaimed God's word (Acts 8:4). This word of God, also called the faith (Acts 13:8), the gospel (I Corinthians 15:1-4), or just the word (Acts 10:36, 37, 44), was preached for (unto) the salvation of lost souls (Acts 9:6; 10:22; 11:14; 22:10). That word was later incorporated into a written message, and came to be known as the New Testament. It, too, like the Old Testament Scriptures, was inspired of God and thus became part of Scripture (II Peter 3:16).

The New Testament, the latter part of that book we call the Bible, was given to be the self-sufficient guide for all Christians after the age of miraculous guidance via the Holy Spirit ended (Ephesians 4:11ff; I Corinthians 13:8). The New Testament itself claims to be from God (II Timothy 3:16). It claims to be "profitable for doctrine, for reproof, for correction, for instruction in righteousness: that the man of God may be perfect, thoroughly furnished unto all good works" (II Timothy 3:16-17).

It also claims that God "hath given unto us all things that pertain unto life and godliness" (II Peter 1:3). It claims the same degree of authority as do the Old Testament Scriptures (Deuteronomy 4:1ff), when it states that man must not go beyond that which is written (I Corinthians 4:6; I Peter 4:11; Revelation 22:18-19), when it claims to be the very words of God (I Corinthians 2:9-13; Ephesians 3:1-4), and when it claims to be the sole means for the salvation of the souls of men (Galatians 1:6-10).

The Bible, therefore, is very much related to the mission and purpose of God the Father, God the Son, and the church which Jesus established. If the Bible is what it claims to be, that is the inspired word of God, then it must of necessity be subject to human understanding. If it is not, then doubts are cast upon (1) the credibility of the Bible, and (2) upon the very nature and existence of God.

It is absolutely essential, therefore, that efforts be made which conclusively demonstrate that the Bible, God's word, is indeed subject to human cognition. Such efforts will necessarily involve argumentation, which was only briefly mentioned in the introduction. To elaborate more fully upon the method of argumentation to be used, it becomes vital that we reiterate the role of the basic argument for Christianity (cf. p. 2).

The basic argument for Christianity entails the following: (1) If we can know that God exists, and if we can know that the Bible is the word of God, and if we can know that the Bible teaches X, where X is any true Bible proposition; then we can know that X is true; (2) we can know that God exists; (3) we can know that the Bible is the word of God; (4) we can know that the Bible teaches X, where X is any true Bible proposition; (5) therefore, we can know that God exists, and that the Bible is the word of God, and that the Bible teaches X, where X is any true Bible proposition; and (6) therefore, we can know that X is true.

If the above argument were set out in symbolic terms (KGE = we can know that God exists, KBWG = we can know that the Bible is the word of God, KBTX = we can know that the Bible teaches X, KX = we can know X is true), it would appear as follows:

(1) (KGE . KBWG . KBTX) > KX
(2) KGE
(3) KBWG
(4) KBTX
(5) (KGE . KBWG . KBTX) (2, 3, 4 Conjunction)
(6) KX (Modus Ponens 1, 5)

This argument is in the form of Modus Ponens, an argument form in which the antecedent is affirmed,³ and in which the consequent follows. This is known to be a valid form of argumentation,⁴ and, if the premises included in such an argument are true, then the argument is labeled "sound."⁵

The force of such an argument is this: (1) if a valid argument form is used, (2) and if the premises of the argument are true, (3) then one is assured of the soundness of the argument, which (4) therefore guarantees the truthfulness of the conclusion. The conclusion of the above argument, in accord with these principles, is that we can **know** X, where X is taught in the Bible, and where X is any true Bible proposition.

This book will not, however, be involved in dealing fully with each premise of the basic argument for Christianity, but will rather devote its primary attention to premise number four. It will be the burden of this work to demonstrate the truthfulness of that premise through the use of sound argumentation.

Closely associated with that argumentation, however, will be arguments relating to the truthfulness of premises two and three. Though this work will not devote itself entirely to strict proofs of these two premises (though they are capable of proof), arguments related to them will be mentioned and discussed as they relate to the proof of premise four.

The Meaning of Premise Four

Before continuing with a discussion of general definitions (chapter 5), presuppositions (chapter 6), limitations (chapter 7), specific examples of the problem (chapter 8), argumentation against hermeneutical agnosticism (chapter 9), argumentation in defense of this thesis (chapter 10), objections considered (chapter 11), an examination of some practical applications (chapter 12), and the conclusion (chapter 13), it is necessary to explicate the meaning of premise four, the premise the truthfulness of which this paper will demonstrate.

Premise four, as mentioned previously, states: We can **KNOW** that the Bible teaches X, where X is any true Bible proposition. What is entailed in that premise is the following:

(1) "We can **KNOW**" means that any person has the ability to come to a cognitive understanding with reference to Bible teachings. To know something is to be certain with reference to the subject known. Thomas B. Warren explains it as follows:

> To say that one has knowledge of, say, a proposition, an object, or a certain state of affairs, is to say that he has such certainty about it that he cannot possibly be wrong about that particular matter.[6]

To claim knowledge with reference to any subject does not indicate arrogance on the part of the one making the claim, if the subject of that knowledge claim is, indeed, capable of human cognition, and if the person making the claim has evidence which yields knowledge of the subject as its conclusion.

(2) When the term "the Bible" is used in this work, it is to be understood to stand for that inspired revelation given by God, through the operation of the Holy Spirit, to apostles, prophets, and other writers of Scripture (I Corinthians 2:9-13; II Peter 1:19-21; Ephesians 3:1-5; II Timothy 3:16-17; et. al.) For the purposes of this work it is assumed that the Bible is verbally inspired, and that all parts of the Bible are equally inspired and inerrant in the autographs. This element relates specifically to premise three in the basic argument for Christianity, and, as with the other premises of that argument, subject to being fully demonstrated.

(3) To say that the Bible "teaches" is to say that the Bible can "impart information"[7] to those who study

it for its meaning and intent.

(4) To say that the Bible teaches X is to say, in a general way, that the Bible is capable of imparting information concerning any of its subjects where that information constitutes a true Bible proposition. It must, of course, be the case that this Bible proposition is subject to human cognition through either explicit statements (i.e., in so many words) or implicit statements (i.e., capable of being deduced from explicit Bible statements). To be a bit more specific, implication involves the following:

> To say that two Biblical statements (say, proposition A and proposition B) imply a third statement (say, proposition C) is to say that it is impossible for both proposition A and proposition B to be true and proposition C not be true. Stated with logical precision, <u>implication</u> means: to say "if proposition X is true, then proposition Y is true," is logically equivalent to saying, "It is impossible for proposition X_8 to be true and proposition Y to be false."

We should not be alarmed that the Bible teaches both explicitly and implicitly. To recognize this is only to respect the manner in which we learn on a day-to-day basis. In the course of our conversations with the people around us we learn by these two methods.

When someone communicates specific information to us (e.g., "It's raining outside."), we are learning from explicit statements. When someone communicates to us implicitly, we gather certain conclusions based upon what they say. For example, if someone tells us "The weatherman said that it would rain today if the temperature drops, and it's dropping" we rightly conclude that rain is imminent.

The Bible communicates in this same way. We learn

specific facts from its specific statements, but we also learn things not specifically mentioned from those same statements.

Consider, for example, the conversion of Saul. The Bible records several accounts of his conversion (cf. Acts 9,22,26), but nowhere in any of these accounts is there a specific statement that tells us that Paul repented. Are we forced to conclude, therefore, that Paul did not repent in order to become a Christian? Certainly not!

We know that no man can become a Christian unless he repents. The Bible is full of injunctions which demand repentance (Luke 13:3; Acts 2:38; 3:19; 17:30; et. al.). If it is necessary for one to repent in order to become a Christian, and if Paul became a Christian, then we rightly conclude that Paul must have repented. We do no injustice to the scripture by making such claims. Indeed, we only claim that which the scriptures claim by doing so.

---

1. Clark Pinnock, Biblical Revelation (Chicago: Moody Press, 1971), p. 209

2. Roy Deaver, How To Study The Bible (Plano, Texas: Biblical Publishing Corporation, 1976), p. 2

3. Lionel Ruby, Logic: An Introduction (Chicago: J.B. Lippincott Company, 1960), p. 275

4. Ibid.

5. Irving M. Copi, Introduction To Logic (New York: Macmillan Publishing Co., Inc., 5th ed., 1978), p. 43

6. Thomas B. Warren, When Is An "Example" Binding? (Jonesboro, Ark.: National Christian Press, 1975), p.33

7. E. Ehrlich, S.B. Flexner, G. Carruth, J.M. Hawkins

(compilers), <u>Oxford American Dictionary</u> (New York: Oxford University Press, 1980), p. 703

8. Warren, <u>When Is An "Example" Binding?</u>, pp. 87-88

CHAPTER FIVE: GENERAL DEFINITIONS

In order to properly understand the development of argumentation given in defense of the thesis, it becomes necessary to describe the meaning of the following key terms: (1) God, (2) the Bible, (3) revelation, (4) inspiration, (5) agnosticism, (6) communication, (7) hermeneutics, (8) logic, (9) the laws of thought, (10) the law of rationality, and (11) epistemology.

The Definition of God

The term "God," as it will be used in this work will designate "a supreme personal being—distinct from the world and creator of the world."[1]

Furthermore,

> The term "God" as used in this series is also in conflict with so-called finitism, the view that God is definitely limited in some attribute such as: power, goodness, knowledge, etc. A deity which is limited by factors which arise outside of his own nature is quite clearly not the source of all reality other than itself (or himself), and is thus not "god" in the sense in which that term will be used by me in these lectures.
> Neither is "God" to be identified with the world nor the world with God, as is done by Pantheists. Pantheism is in conflict with the view that God is the source of the world and thus transcends the world.
> And it is clear that "theism" as I use it here, is in conflict with the view that there is only one existent, the absolute,

> with this one existent being the true subject of all significant propositions. "God," as used by me in these lectures, is the source of the world and is thus not all that exists.
>
> When I use the word "God" I shall be referring to that eternal, self-existent being who is infinite in all of his attributes: infinite in power, infinite in love and goodness, infinite in knowledge and wisdom, infinite in presence, etc.[2]

In addition to these characteristics, it must be noted that the term "God," as will be used in this work, does not refer to a "God of process."

> Further, being infinite in his nature, he cannot change in quality. This is clear for the following reasons: If he changed for the better, this would mean that prior to the change he was less good than after the change and so was less than infinite in the matter in which the change occurred. If he changed for the worse, this would mean that after the change he was less good than before the change and became less than infinite. Obviously, neither of these will do if God is infinite.[3]

The Definition Of The Bible

As mentioned previously, when the expression "the Bible" is used in this work, it is to be understood to stand for that inspired revelation given by God, through the operation of the Holy Spirit, to apostles, prophets, and other inspired writers of Scripture (I Corinthians 2:9-13; II Peter 1:19-21; Ephesians 3:1-4; II Timothy 3:16-17; et. al.). For the purposes of this work it is assumed that the Bible is inspired word for word, and that all parts of the Bible are equally inspired. Furthermore, the Bible, as written in the autographs (original writings) is assumed to be totally inerrant. These elements relate directly to premise three of the basic argument for Christianity, and, as the other premises of that argument, subject to being fully demonstrated.

The Definition of Revelation

As it will be used in the remainder of this work, the term "revelation" will be understood to mean "an objective disclosure of truth by God, and used in contrast to illumination, which is the subjective understanding of a revelation."[4]
The importance of the objective nature of revelation is emphasized by J. D. Thomas in the following remarks:

> When we say that the Bible is God's revelation, we are saying that it consists of a propositional message, sent from God's mind to man's mind, and that it is intellectually knowable and thus logically understandable. Also we should understand that the revelation is clear-cut, definite and objective so that there need be no vagueness or misunderstanding whatever. Unless the message God is revealing can be known exactly, the revelation has failed of its purpose and really is no revelation.[5]

The Definition of Inspiration

The term "inspiration" as used in this work will be understood to mean:

- 21 -

> ...the Divinely determined products of inspired men; the Bib. writers are called inspired as breathed into by the Holy Spirit, so that the product of their activities transcends human powers and becomes Divinely authoritative. Inspiration is, therefore, usually defined as a supernatural influence exerted on the sacred writers by the Spirit of God, by virtue of which their writings are given Divine trustworthiness.[6]

It is important to note that the Bible itself claims to be inspired of God (II Timothy 3:16). Furthermore, the Bible claims to have originated through the operation of the Holy Spirit of God (II Peter 1:19-21). The Bible also claims to be inspired to the level of the words used by the individual writers (I Corinthians 2:9-13; Ephesians 3:1-5). Finally, the extent of inspiration applies to all Scripture with equal degree (II Timothy 3:13; Psalm 119:160).

The Definition of Agnosticism

The term "agnosticism" originated having exclusive reference to the question of God's existence,[7] but the term as used philosophically has wider application. Robert Flint in his book entitled <u>Agnosticism</u> explains the broader use of the term when he says: "It is a view or theory as to what man can and cannot know--as to the inherent and constitutive limits of cognition."[8]

Flint goes on to explain the theory of agnosticism and its impact upon theology and other disciplines:

> The term agnosticism then is, in my opinion, only accurately and appropriately employed when regarded as equivalent for

what has been variously called philosophical, or theoretical, or metaphysical scepticism, or simply scepticism. It is the theory of the nature and limits of human intelligence which questions either the certainty of all knowledge and the veracity of every mental power, or the certainty of some particular kind of knowledge and the veracity of some particular mental power or powers. The limitation of the word to the sphere of religion is quite unjustifiable. There is no reason for calling a man an agnostic merely because he is an atheist or a positivist or a materialist. The name is appropriate, indeed, to one whose refusal to believe in the existence of God and of spiritual things is rested on the ground that the human mind is inherently and constitutionally incapable of knowing whether there are a God and spiritual things or not. But there is no kind of truth which may not be rejected on the ground that the human mind is inherently and constitutionally incapable of ascertaining whether or not there is such truth.[9]

Flint, therefore, indicates that the term "agnosticism," though originating with the question of God's existence, is correctly applied to any discipline in which the conclusion yields "doubt or disbelief of some or all of the powers of knowing possessed by the human mind."[10]

With reference to the thesis of this work, the term "agnosticism" is applied to the discipline of Biblical interpretation, commonly styled hermeneutics. As it is applied to hermeneutics, agnosticism affirms that we cannot know that any given meaning or interpretation

- 23 -

of the Bible is true.[11]

Agnosticism entails an approach akin to subjectivism. A plethora of interpretations results, and there is no way, given the tenets of hermeneutical agnosticism, to ascertain the truth or the falsity of any of them.[12]

The Definition Of Communication

The third premise of the basic argument for Christianity is directly involved in the problem of God's revelation of his will to mankind. That premise states that the Bible is the word of God... that it is God's communication to man.

The premise with which this paper deals, however, is also related to the question of communication. It does not deal so much with the means and method of communication, or whether or not such communications occurred (though such is presumed), but rather whether or not such communication can be understood by man.

It is essential, then, to understand the meaning of the term "communication." Robert Cathcart says: "Communication is a word that describes the process of transferring meaning from one individual to another. Through the communication process, we interpret reality and select alternate paths of behavior."[13]

Both Rudolph Verderber and William Schramm concur with Cathcart's emphasis upon the transfer of meaning. Verderber defines communication as "<u>the process of stimulating meaning</u>."[14]

Schramm states that: "<u>Communication</u> comes from the Latin <u>communis</u>, common. When we communicate we are trying to establish a 'commonness' with someone. That is, we are trying to share information, an idea, or an attitude."[15]

To say, therefore, that God has communicated with man is to say: (1) that God is capable of communication with man, (2) that man can recognize what that communication is, and (3) that man can

- 24 -

understand the meaning and intent of that communication.

The Definition of Hermeneutics

There are numerous definitions which might be given for the term "hermeneutics," but Bernard Ramm provides the essence of many of them when he quite simply states that "Hermeneutics is the science and art of Biblical interpretation."[16] But, because this definition is so simplistic and brief, it lacks something with regard to the true nature and perspective of hermeneutics.

To learn something about the role of hermeneutics as it relates to other disciplines of Biblical scholarship, the following lengthy quotation from Milton S. Terry is given.

> Biblical Hermeneutics, having a specific field of its own, should be carefully distinguished from other branches of theological science with which it is often and quite naturally associated. It is to be distinguished from Biblical Introduction, Textual Criticism, and Exegesis. Biblical Introduction, or Isagogics, is devoted to the historico-critical examination of the different books of the Bible. It inquires after their age, authorship, genuineness, and canonical authority, tracing at the same time their origin, preservation, and integrity, and exhibiting their contents, relative rank, and general character and value. The scientific treatment of these several subjects is often called "Higher Criticism." Textual Criticism has for its special object the ascertaining of the exact words of the original texts of the sacred books. Its method of procedure is

to collate and compare ancient manuscripts, ancient versions, and ancient scripture quotations, and, by careful and discriminating judgment, sift conflicting testimony, weigh the evidence of all kinds, and thus endeavour to determine the true reading of every doubtful text. This science is often called the "Lower Criticism." Where such criticism ends, Hermeneutics properly begins, and aims to establish the principles, methods, and rules which are needful to unfold the sense of what is written. Its object is to elucidate whatever may be obscure or ill-defined, so that every reader may be able, by an intelligent process, to obtain the exact ideas intended by the author. Exegesis is the application of these principles and laws, the actual bringing out into formal statement, and by other terms, the meaning of the author's words. Exegesis is related to hermeneutics as preaching is to homiletics, or, in general, as practice is to theory. Exposition is another word often used synonymously with exegesis, and has essentially the same signification; and yet, perhaps, in common usage, exposition denotes a more extended development and illustration of the sense, dealing more largely with other scriptures by comparison and contrast.[17]

Though Terry states that the relationship between hermeneutics and exegesis is parallel to that between theory and practice, it must be noted that hermeneutics is not entirely theoretical.

> But while we are careful to distinguish hermeneutics from these kindred branches of exegetical theology, we should not fail

to note that a science of interpretation must essentially depend on exegesis for the maintenance and illustration of its principles and rules. As the full grammar of a language establishes its principles by sufficient examples and by formal praxis, so a science of hermeneutics must needs verify and illustrate its principles by examples of their practical application. Its province is not merely to define principles and methods, but also to exemplify and illustrate them. Hermeneutics, therefore, is both a science and an art. As a science, it enunciates principles, investigates the laws of thought and language, and classifies its facts and results. As an art, it teaches what application these principles should have, and establishes their soundness by showing their practical value in the elucidation of the more difficult scriptures. The hermeneutical art thus cultivates and establishes a valid exegetical procedure.[18]

It can be readily seen, then, that the principles and practice of hermeneutics are intricately involved in the fourth premise of the basic argument for Christianity.

The Definition Of Logic

According to Lionel Ruby, logic is "defined as the science of valid inference. Logic is the study of the principles that determine whether inferences are justified or unjustified."[19]

In like manner, Thomas Warren defines logic as "that discipline which attempts to determine whether conclusions are warranted from given evidence."[20]

The Definition Of The Laws Of Thought

The laws of thought will be alluded to several times throughout the remainder of this work. It is, therefore, fitting that they should be explained.

The laws of thought are usually understood to refer to the following: the Principle of Identity, the Principle of Contradiction, and the Principle of Excluded Middle.[21]

Their meanings are as follows:

> The principle of Identity asserts that **if any statement is true, then it is true.** The Principle of Contradiction asserts that **no statement can be both true and false.** The Principle of Excluded Middle asserts that **any statement is either true or false.**[22]

In symbolic terms these laws are represented in the following terminology:

> In the terminology of the present chapter, we may rephrase them as follows. The Principle of Identity asserts that every statement of the form $p \supset p$ is true, that is, that every such statement is a tautology. The Principle of Contradiction asserts that every statement of the form $p \cdot \neg p$ is false, that is, that every such statement is self contradictory. The Principle of Excluded Middle asserts that every statement of the form $p \vee \neg p$ is true, that is, that every such statement is a tautology.[23]

The Definition Of The Law Of Rationality

Lionel Ruby defines the law of rationality in the following manner: "Every person who is interested in logical thinking accepts what we shall call the 'law of rationality,' which may be stated as follows: **We ought to justify our conclusions by adequate evidence.**"[24] The law of rationality, also called the law of sufficient reason, can also be stated in this way: "one should draw only such conclusions as are warranted by the evidence."[25]

The Definition Of Epistemology

Epistemology is generally regarded to mean "theory of knowledge," due mainly to the literal meaning of the word, but it involves much more than that. "Epistemology, or the theory of knowledge, is that branch of philosophy which is concerned with the nature and scope of knowledge, its presuppositions and basis, and the general reliability of claims to knowledge."[26]

Epistemology, therefore, is involved specifically in the attempt to provide solutions to numerous problems relating to knowledge. The main problem with which this branch of philosophy is concerned is the very possibility of knowledge. Ledger Wood says: "The initial and inescapable problem with which the epistemologist is confronted is that of the very **possibility of knowledge:** Is genuine knowledge at all attainable?"[27]

In addition to the possibility of knowledge, the field of epistemology is also concerned with the limits of knowledge. Wood further says: "An epistemologist who rejects an extreme or agnostic scepticism, may very properly seek to determine the limits of knowledge and to assert that genuine knowledge is, within certain prescribed limits, possible yet beyond those limits impossible."[28]

The subject of epistemology is extremely important with regard to the basic thesis of this work. That thesis states that it is indeed possible to **know** that the Bible teaches those things **necessary** for our soul's **salvation,** and that we, that is to say, all men, can come to **knowledge** of those elements of the Bible's teaching.

There are several distinct views with reference to the possibility of man's having knowledge of the Bible, but only one of them accurately represents the Bible's view. Some of those views are illustrated by the following diagrams:

VIEW #1

SUBJECTS OF BIBLE TEACHING

a b c d e f g h i j k l m n

knowable not knowable

VIEW #2

SUBJECTS OF BIBLE TEACHING

a b c d e f g h i j k l m n

knowable greater degree knowable lesser degree

VIEW #3

SUBJECTS OF BIBLE TEACHING

$\underbrace{\text{a b c d e f g h i j k l m n}}$

not subject to human knowledge

VIEW #4

SUBJECTS OF BIBLE TEACHING

$\underbrace{\text{a b c d e f g h i j k l m n}}$

completely subject to human knowledge

 Hermeneutical agnosticism would espouse either view #1 or view #3. View #1 is that view which maintains that some elements of the Bible's teaching can be known (i.e., understood with certainty), but that there remain those elements which cannot be understood with any degree of certainty whatsoever. View #3 denies the possibility, and therefore the certainty, of <u>any</u> (i.e., all) Bible knowledge.
 In opposition to those views are views #2 and #4. View #2 entails that there are elements of the Bible's teaching which can be extremely well understood, but that there also are elements which can be understood, but not to the same degree as that of the first class. To illustrate, **if** the total teaching of the Bible were limited to ten subjects, view #2 would maintain that we could have thorough knowledge of six to eight of them, with a lesser knowledge of two to four of them.
 View #4 is that view which asserts that all subjects of the Bible's teaching are equally well understood, that is to say, that man can understand everything there is to understand about the Bible. I know of no one who

maintains such a position.

It is the position of this work that view #2 more closely represents the Bible's view of epistemology than does any other view. In order to more accurately depict the Bible's view, it might be necessary to include additional graduated degrees ranging from the least amount of knowledge possible to the greatest amount of knowledge possible. View #2 maintains that **every** Bible teaching is subject, at the very least, to **some degree of understanding**. Furthermore, this view entails that there are those subjects taught in the Bible about which we might have a much greater degree of knowledge. To be certain, if we have any knowledge of any Bible teaching, we can say that that knowledge is certain. But, that is not to say that we know absolutely everything there is to know about the specific subject, but rather that the amount which we do know is still known absolutely, that is with certainty.

Though further discussion will ensue relative to this facet of the thesis, it is important to point out the criterion whereby the epistemological position described above is made. Quite simply put, it is this: If a particular Bible teaching is **necessary** to be understood for the **salvation** of man's soul, then that particular teaching **can be understood**. If a particular Bible teaching is **not necessary** (i.e., not essential) to be understood for the salvation of man's soul, then that teaching **may** or **may not** be understood. The decision regarding which teachings are, or are not, necessary to be understood for the salvation of the souls of men is not left to man. As we will note further, the Bible plainly teaches which teachings are absolutely essential and which are not.

---

1. F.C. Copleston in Bertrand Russell and F.C. Copleston, "A Debate On The Existence of God" in <u>The Existence Of God</u> ed. by John Hick (New York:

Macmillan Publishing Co., Inc., 1964), p. 167

2. Thomas B. Warren, Have Atheists Proved There Is No God? (Jonesboro, Ark.: National Christian Press, 1972), pp. vi-vii

3. Ibid., p. 25

4. Norman L. Geisler and William E. Nix, A General Introduction To The Bible (Chicago: Moody Press, 1968), p. 454

5. J.D. Thomas, Heaven's Window (Abilene, Texas: Biblical Research Press, 1974), p. 4

6. Benjamin B. Warfield, "Inspiration" in International Standard Bible Encyclopedia-Volume III ed. by James Orr (Grand Rapids: William B. Eerdmans Publishing Company, 1956, reprinted 1978), p. 1473

7. cf. p.1, fn. 1

8. Flint, Agnosticism, p. 1

9. Ibid., pp. 22-23

10. Ibid., p. 17

11. "Agnosticism" is not to be confused with "gnosticism." The latter emphasizes an esoteric and elitist form of knowledge beyond the normal range of belief, while the former denies specific elements of knowledge which actually fall within the normal range of belief.

12. It is imperative to note that hermeneutical agnosticism can be maintained "across the board," and thus held with reference to all of the Bible's teachings, or it can be held with reference to specific Bible teachings. Either way, the consequences remain the

same.

13. Robert Cathcart, *Post Communication: Criticism And Evaluation* (Indianapolis: The Bobbs-Merrill Company, Inc., 1966), p. 1

14. Rudolph F. Verderber, *Communicate!* (Belmont, California: Wadsworth Publishing Company, Inc., 1975), p. 4

15. Wilbur Schramm, "How Communication Works" in *Communication: Concepts And Processes* ed. by Joseph A. DeVito (Englewood Cliffs, N.J.: Prentice-Hall, Inc., rev. and enl. 1976), p. 11

16. Bernard Ramm, *Protestant Biblical Interpretation* (Grand Rapids: Baker Book House, 3rd rev. ed., 1970), p. 1

17. Milton S. Terry, *Biblical Hermeneutics* (Grand Rapids: Zondervan Publishing House, 4th printing, 1976), p. 19

18. Ibid., p. 20

19. Ruby, *Logic: An Introduction*, p. viii

20. Warren, *When Is An "Example" Binding?*, p. 19

21. Copi, *Introduction To Logic*, p. 306

22. Ibid.

23. Ibid., pp. 306-307

24. Ruby, *Logic: An Introduction*, p. 131

25. Warren, *When Is An "Example" Binding?*, p. 21

26. D.W. Hamlyn, "History of Epistemology" in *The*

Encyclopedia Of Philosophy-Volume III ed. by Paul Edwards (New York: Macmillan Publishing Company, Inc. and The Free Press, 1967), p. 8-9

27. Ledger Wood, "Epistemology" in Dictionary Of Philosophy ed. by Dagobert D. Runes (Totowa, N.J.: Littlefield, Adams and Company, 1962 ed.), p. 94

28. Ibid.

CHAPTER SIX: PRESUPPOSITIONS

In order to better facilitate the development of the thesis, it is$_1$ essential to note the following presuppositions:

(1) For the purpose of this work it is assumed that God exists, that he is wholly personal, that he is infinite in all of his attributes, and that such is capable of demonstration through logical argumentation. Though it is not the primary thrust of this work to prove the existence of God, such argumentation will be presented later as it relates to the basic thesis.

(2) It is assumed that the Bible is the word of God, and that it reveals the will of God for man. Though this facet is intrinsically related to the thesis, argumentation will be presented in its defense only as it relates to the thesis. The necessity of this action will become evident as actual formal argumentation and discussion of the thesis occurs.

(3) It will be taken as self-evident that the laws of thought (identity, excluded middle, and non-contradiction) are recognized as true.

(4) Furthermore, it is assumed that the law of rationality is recognized as being axiomatic.

(5) In addition to these assumptions, it is to be assumed that knowledge is actually possible, and that the scepticism generally employed to attack the foundations of epistemology actually comprises a tacit admission that such an assumption is warranted.

With regard to the limits of knowledge, the only proposition to be thoroughly discussed (and affirmed) is that the limits imposed by the hermeneutical agnostic are much too confining according to both$_2$ the Biblical view and this work's view of epistemology.

It must be mentioned, that though each of these presuppositions is to be employed in defense of the thesis, each assumption is in itself capable of demonstration. Though a full proof and discussion of each is not the burden of this thesis, each will be discussed as it relates to the thrust of this work.

---

1. To presuppose is simply to imply as an antecedent fact. All of the presuppositions cited within this chapter are capable of logical and/or empirical demonstration, and thus not equivalent to fideistic presuppositions.

2. It is the firm conviction of the writer that the view presented herein is, indeed, an accurate portrayal of the Biblical view.

CHAPTER SEVEN: LIMITATIONS

A discussion and defense of this book's thesis will, of necessity, be composed of numerous facets of argumentation. Those arguments will touch upon many different subjects, but all of them will be discussed as they relate to the defense of the thesis. To delineate between those tangential subjects and the thesis, the following list of limitations is supplied:

(1) **This work will not be a textbook on the existence of God, nor will it provide extensive argumentation yielding the conclusion that God does exist.** That proposition, though an intricate element of the thesis, is assumed to be true. Arguments relating to it are only given for the purpose of demonstrating that we can know that the Bible teaches X, where X is any true Bible proposition subject to cognition.

(2) **This work will not be thoroughly devoted to proving that the Bible is the word of God.** That premise is assumed for the purpose of this work, though it will be an important element in the defense of the thesis. The argumentation that will be given concerning the truthfulness of this proposition will be presented only to buttress the argumentation for the thesis.

(3) **It is not within the scope of this work to demonstrate that the Bible is the only God-given revelation for mankind.** In other words, this pursuit will not involve itself in argumentation which proves that the book of Mormon, the Koran, or any other work is solely of human origin and therefore not a revelation from God. For the purpose of this work, it is assumed that the Bible constitutes the sole revelation from God available to man. That proposition, though assumed for this work, is, indeed, capable of demonstrable proof.

(4) **This effort will not constitute an extensive treatise on epistemology.** A thorough attempt to demonstrate the possibility and/or the limits of

knowledge will not be made. Epistemology will only be discussed as it relates to the possibility and the limits of Bible knowledge. The material to be presented later will only deal with limited argumentation to show conclusively that knowledge, in general, is possible, and thus, that Biblical knowledge is possible.

(5) Given the possibility of knowledge, **it will be the purpose of this work to demonstrate that we can KNOW that the Bible teaches specific propositions, and that we can KNOW THE MEANING AND INTENT of those propositions, ESPECIALLY AS THEY RELATE TO THE SALVATION OF MANKIND.**

It **will not**, however, be the goal of this work to prove that we can **know all that there is to know** about any specific subject. Even the casual Bible student knows that the Bible contains some really difficult topics, but though such topics as the incarnation of Christ and the indwelling of the Holy Spirit are, indeed, difficult Bible topics, it is the contention of this endeavor that we can know some things, but **certainly not everything** (as God knows everything), relative to those, or any other, Bible subjects.

The basic thrust of this work is that the knowledge that is **humanly attainable** about these Bible subjects **is sufficient to enable man to be obedient to the will of God and to obtain salvation by his grace through our faith.** This work, then, **will not attempt** to demonstrate that we can know and understand everything that the Bible teaches about all Bible subjects, **nor will it attempt** to demonstrate that we can know all that there is to know about any one Bible subject (as God knows all that there is to know).

(6) **Though different Bible passages will be discussed throughout the course of this project, no attempt will be made to provide a complete commentary on every difficult passage, alleged discrepancy, and supposed contradiction.** The passages to be discussed will be incorporated into this work for the purpose of defending the thesis or for consideration as possible

objections to the truthfulness of that thesis.

(7) **This effort will not engage in the discussion of material relative to the subject of textual criticism.** For the purpose of this work, it is assumed that the Bible as we have it accurately represents the word of God as initially given to man.

(8) **Though the subject of hermeneutics and Biblical interpretation is at the very heart of this work, this project will not be a textbook on the subject which deals with a listing of numerous principles and methods to be incorporated in the science of interpretation.** Rather, this work has as its very function the investigation into the **possibility of hermeneutics.** Those principles, methods, and rules mentioned and discussed will be used only as they contribute to the defense of the basic thesis.

(9) **Bible passages will be discussed which, at least on the surface, seem to contradict the thesis of this endeavor.** Due to the enormity of the number of passages which **could be considered,** it will be impossible to study all of them. Those passages which will be studied are to be understood as being representative of those which will not be discussed.

Beginning with the following section of this work the basic problem will be exemplified. That section will be followed by argumentation against agnosticism and argumentation in support of the thesis, objections to the thesis, some practical considerations, and the conclusion of the work.

CHAPTER EIGHT: EXAMPLES OF THE PROBLEM

Up to this point agnosticism has only been discussed "from a distance." We noted its realm of influence in the first chapter. We detailed its consequences in the second chapter. It becomes essential, therefore, that we study some specific examples of hermeneutical agnosticism.

By analyzing these examples we will see firsthand the nature of agnosticism in Biblical interpretation, and thus understand more fully the import of the hermeneutical agnostic's claims.

The application of the principles of hermeneutical agnosticism is widespread. In addition to manifesting itself in the different Biblical interpretations of the religions of the world, agnosticism makes itself known in varying interpretations within the true church of Christ.

Agnosticism in the Lord's church is seen in: (1) the problem concerning marriage, divorce, and remarriage, (2) the distinction between faith and reason, and the roles of each, (3) the differences held regarding the Biblical doctrine of fellowship, (4) the problems centering around the question of the role and authority of elders in the church, (5) the problem of religious unity, (6) the differences between faith and opinion, and numerous other Bible subjects.

In order to illustrate the agnostic position as it relates to the above (and other) issues, let us note the following examples. These three examples were gathered from different writers in different parts of the nation, but all of them are related.[1]

The first example exhibits a very broad-based agnosticism. The second example manifests a very narrowly focused agnosticism in that it only directs itself toward one issue, marriage, divorce, and remarriage. The third example expresses the ultimate logical consequences of the first two examples.

Example One

The first example deals with the certainty of human knowledge. In an article entitled "I Know I'm Right!," Joe Beam speaks about a denominational "pastor" who was so sure he (i.e., the "pastor") knew the exact date of the "rapture."

Beam was impressed with the sincerity and the diligence which this "pastor" exhibited as he taught about the coming "rapture." The time came, however, and the "rapture" did not occur, yet Beam could not doubt the sincerity with which this man interpreted the Scriptures. With respect to this Beam said:

> Why do I consider him an object lesson? The answer by now is pretty obvious. If a sincere, zealous man can so misunderstand the word of God as did he, then there is a possibility I can do the same thing. He could never see his error because his mind was closed. The same would be true of any of us. Now every time that I'm inclined to reject another man's view or argument because I've already made up my mind, I remember this poor, arrogant man. I know that having a conviction and sharing it with others is not necessarily antithetical to open mindedness. I don't want to vacillate with every wind that blows. That's spiritual immaturity (Eph. 4:14). Neither do I want to be ever learning and never coming to a knowledge of the truth (2 Tim. 3:7). But neither do I want to be more loyal to what I already believe than I am to truth (2 Thess. 2:10-12). What I want to believe or am comfortable in believing is no substitute for loving and desiring what truth actually is. To really

love truth means an open mind to it and to the possibility of my having misunderstood it. Exclusively (sic) and fanaticism will hardly serve me well in that effort.²

Though Beam does not explicitly state it, he does seem to be hinting that it is impossible to know, absolutely and with certainty, the truth regarding what the Bible teaches about any subject. He does not set out a formal argument, but he appears to be working along these lines:
(1) If man is fallible with respect to "knowledge", then man can be wrong with respect to "knowledge" (e.g., Bible knowledge).
(2) If man can be wrong with respect to "knowledge," then man can not be sure of truth.
(3) Man is fallible with respect to "knowledge."
(4) If man is fallible with respect to "knowledge," then man can not be sure of truth.
(5) Man cannot be sure of the truth.

Put into symbolic terms (Hf = man is fallible with respect to "knowledge," Hw = man can be wrong with respect to "knowledge," St = men can be sure of truth), the above argument would be as follows:

(1) Hf > Hw
(2) Hw > -St
(3) Hf
(4) Hf > -St (1, 2 Hypothetical Syllogism)
(5) -St (4, 3 Modus Ponens)

The argument, though valid in form, contains false premises (i.e., premises two and four), and is, therefore, an unsound argument. Beam has, therefore, tentatively argued that he is not sure of any of his beliefs concerning the Bible, or that they are, at the very least, subject to doubt and scrutiny. But, upon closer examination, even his very argument is suspect.
Note the following argument which could be made to

demonstrate that Beam's conclusion is suspect:

(1) If man cannot be sure of the truth, then Beam cannot be sure that his second premise (cf. above) is true.

(2) Man cannot be sure of the truth. (Assuming the conclusion of Beam's alleged argument.)

(3) Therefore, Beam cannot be sure that his second premise is true.

Put into symbolic terms (St = man can be sure of the truth, Hw = human beings can be wrong with reference to knowledge), the preceding argument would be as follows:

(1) -St > -(Hw > -St)
(2) -St (Beam's conclusion)
(3) -(Hw > -St) (1, 2 Modus Ponens)

The argument is valid in form (Modus Ponens) and, given the supposed truthfulness of Beam's initial conclusion, it also contains true premises. If such is the case, then Beam **cannot even be sure that he is not sure** about human cognitive ability, which, to say the least, places him in the midst of the agnostic camp. It would be ridiculous, therefore, not to mention inconsistent, for Beam to **maintain that he cannot be sure of any Bible knowledge**, but that he **is sure that he cannot be sure** of any Bible knowledge. Such a position is untenable.

An additional argument, from the positive side, demonstrates that it is indeed possible to be certain with regard to knowledge. Note the following:

(1) If Jesus said that it was possible for man to know the truth, then it is possible for man to know and be sure of the truth.

(2) Jesus said it was possible for man to know the truth.

(3) It is possible, therefore, for man to know and be sure of the truth.

Put into symbolic terms (Jkt = Jesus said that it was possible for man to know the truth, St = it is possible for man to know and be sure of the truth), the above argument would be as follows:

(1) Jkt > St
(2) Jkt (cf. John 8:32)
(3) St (1, 2 Modus Ponens)

The above argument is Modus Ponens in form, and is, therefore, valid. Furthermore, the premises of the argument are true, resulting in a sound argument.$_3$ By means of this argument, and the preceding one, we have shown: (1) that Beam's argument was positing agnosticism, and (2) that it really is possible to know and be sure of truth, therefore showing Beam's conclusion to be false.

This example has proven to be exactly like those mentioned in the second chapter of this work (cf. pp. 3-6) In order to prove his position, Joe Beam needed to know a certain proposition, which he denied could be known. His position, therefore, could not be substantiated, and is therefore subject to disbelief.

On the other hand, knowing that given propositions can be subject to human cognition has allowed this writer to demonstrate that Beam's conclusion was false and that the opposite conclusion could be correctly drawn.

Example Two

The previous discussion of the problem of agnosticism in the Lord's church dealt with a very general element of that position, but the agnostic position is often maintained relative to a single Biblical teaching as opposed to all Bible teachings.

To be sure, the general position of agnosticism, which presumes that we can not be sure of **any Bible teaching, seems to be the most dangerous.** But, if an agnostic position is maintained **even with respect to a SINGLE Bible teaching,** the consequences **can be the** same.[4]

Joe Beam, through his article, **cast doubt upon the certainty of any Bible truth.** His agnostic position, therefore, was very **general** in nature. The following example, however, demonstrates that agnosticism can be applied to a specific (i.e., single) area of Bible knowledge, and yet result in the same consequences as a more general form of agnosticism.

In the January 6, 1981 issue of the FIRM FOUNDATION, the following article entitled "Must We Divide?" appeared by Rubel Shelly. In this article Shelly advances hermeneutical agnosticism relative to the Bible's teaching on marriage, divorce, and remarriage.[5]

> The elements of division are appearing again in our brotherhood. This time the issue is not premillennialism or orphan's homes but <u>divorce and remarriage</u>.
>
> I have strong convictions to the effect that only such persons as have put away fornicators have the right to marry again following divorce. Those who divorce for a trivial cause or who are responsible for breaking a marriage commitment through sexual infidelity are, on my understanding of the Scripture, guilty of the sin of adultery if they remarry. I have elsewhere argued this case from the Bible and am convinced it is correct.
>
> The purpose of this article, however, is not to argue the issue of divorce and remarriage further but to <u>appeal for cooler heads among disputants in the matter and to sound a warning against dividing the church over this issue.</u>
>
> Brethren with equally sincere motives and demonstrated concern for the kingdom of God hold views contrary to my own. We cannot both be right. And much serious, prayerful, and diligent study needs

- 46 -

to be done in an effort to come to unity of belief among us.

My intellective powers are not infallible, and I may be wrong about what the Bible teaches on divorce and remarriage. I must maintain a calm and reasonable spirit while studying through this difficult subject. Of course, those with a contrary view are not claiming infallibility either; and the willingness to reconsider the merits/demerits of a view is a virtue which persons on both sides of the matter must exhibit. <u>Only the Word of God is infallible</u>, and we are seeking to come to agreement about its teaching on a subject everyone admits to be challenging—both intellectually and practically.

Let egos be restrained. Let voices be lowered. Let abusive <u>ad</u> <u>hominem</u> arguments cease. Let threats and talk of disfellowship be discontinued.

Let us accept the fact that we are in a time of study, discussion and inquiry.

We have managed to live with one another for decades in disagreement on this topic—as well as the war question, the indwelling of the Holy Spirit, etc. There is no reason to divide the church over it now—unless we degenerate to the carnal state of the Corinthians and resort to choosing up sides by the names of our champions. God forbid that we should do so!

We should never have divided over the issues mentioned in the first paragraph of this article. May we show more maturity and love for the body of Christ than to rip it asunder over this one.[6]

- 47 -

Shelly has not specifically formulated any argument in this article, but several propositions related to an argument were made. Note the following propositions in symbolic terms (X = the truth of the Bible's teaching on marriage, divorce, and remarriage, and the position which Shelly says he is "convinced...is correct."):

(1) X (cf. para. 2—"I have elsewhere...correct.")
(2) -X (cf. para. 5—"My intellective powers are...")
(3) -(X . -X) (cf. para. 4—"We cannot both be right.")
(4) X . -X (1, 2 conjunction)

The importance of the above four propositions may not be immediately evident, thus an explanation is in order.

Given "X" as the truth of the Bible's teaching on the subject of marriage, divorce, and remarriage, the position which Shelly says "is correct," then the following is seen from his article: (1) Shelly believes, is convinced, and has argued that his position is the Bible position (proposition 1 above);

(2) Shelly is not so "sure" with respect to his position that he would say it is absolutely true (proposition 2 above);

(3) Shelly realizes that his position, and the opposite of his position, cannot both be right (proposition 3 above); and

(4) through the logical move known as conjunction, in which two premises that are true are "added" to form another new premise which states that both premises are true, we see that Shelly is sure **AND** that Shelly is not sure.

The distressing problem is that Shelly's statement that his position and the opposing position cannot both be right (proposition 3 above) is in direct opposition to the conjunction of his statements (propositions 1 and 2) when conjoined (proposition 4). **HE HAS THUS AFFIRMED AND DENIED THE SAME PROPOSITION (X**

. -X) WITHIN HIS ARTICLE!
The upshot of this is that Shelly, by affirming two opposing propositions, is affirming a logical contradiction, and thus affirming that any proposition can be both true and false at the same time. This scepticism is, as Robert Flint has mentioned, equivalent to agnosticism.

As stated previously, there is no real argument based upon these propositions, but the following argument could be made which shows that Shelly is indeed correct in his convictions. (X = the truth of the Bible's teaching on marriage, divorce, and remarriage, and the position which Shelly says he is "convinced...is correct", LC(co) = the law of Christ is for Christians only, NC(na) = non-Christians are not amenable to the law of Christ, and NCG(lh) = non-Christian Gentiles are under the law on the heart)[7]

(1) X v -X (law of excluded middle)
(2) -X > [LC(co) . NC(na) . NCG(lh) . etc.]
(3) -[LC(co) . NC(na) . NCG(lh) . etc.]
(4) —X (2, 3 Modus Tollens)
(5) X (4 Double Negation; 1,4 Disjunctive Syllogism)

The previous argument would read as follows:
(1) Either the Bible's teaching on marriage, divorce, and remarriage IS TRUE OR the Bible's teaching on marriage, divorce, and remarriage IS NOT TRUE.
(2) If the Bible's teaching on marriage, divorce, and remarriage is **not true,** then the law of Christ is for Christians only, and non-Christians are not amenable to the law of Christ, and non-Christian Gentiles are under the law on the heart, etc.
(3) It is **NOT** the case that the law of Christ is for Christians only, and that non-Christians are not amenable to the law of Christ, and that non-Christian Gentiles are under the law on the heart.
(4) Therefore, it is the case that it is false to say the the Bible's position on marriage, divorce, and remarriage is false.

(5) Therefore, the Bible's position on marriage, divorce, and remarriage is true.

The above argument demonstrates that the teaching of the Bible regarding marriage, divorce, and remarriage is true, and that we can know that the teaching of the Bible on this subject is true.[8] The argument demonstrates the conclusion which Shelly says he has argued for, and which he is "convinced...is correct." If this is true, and given the statements of Shelly it is, why does he then advocate such an equivocal and agnostic position in the article "Must We Divide?"

Shelly is no foreigner to the discipline of logic and its application to the realm of Christian evidences and apologetics. In his book What Shall We Do With The Bible?, Shelly stated the following:

> It is felt that this book is unique in that it offers not only a number of facts relevant to the subject of inspiration and authority of the Bible but also presents the logical tool which demonstrates that these facts demand the conclusion that the Bible is from God. .... only when the facts are presented within the framework of a valid argument is any conclusion justified and established.[9]

In the same book, Shelly further states:

> The Bible is the Word of God! This I hold not by a "leap of faith" (i.e. beyond what the "hard evidence" demands as a conclusion) but on the basis of evidence which demands that Scripture be so regarded. This is not merely a "more reasonable view" of the Bible than any other; it is the only possible view in light of the evidence at hand.[10]

In the article previously cited ("Must We Divide?"), Shelly stated that his "intellective powers are not infallible, and I may be wrong about what the Bible teaches on divorce and remarriage." Elsewhere, in the same article, he said that he had "argued this case from the Bible and am convinced it is correct." How does one reconcile this last statement with the prior statement regarding Shelly's intellective infallibility? Recognizing his intellectual infallibility, he yet was "convinced" of the correctness of a given conclusion. But, given the basic thrust of the article "Must We Divide?," is Shelly ever justified in being "convinced" of anything?

If his convictions with regard to marriage, divorce, and remarriage are the products of the same logical process of reasoning which he so boldly spoke about in his book <u>What Shall We Do With The Bible?</u>, why is it that he is so certain concerning the inspiration and authority of the Bible, but seemingly so uncertain regarding the truthfulness of his position on marriage, divorce, and remarriage? Does the discipline of logic yield absolute and certain conclusions within the realm of the inspiration and authority of the Bible, but falter when it comes to actually interpreting the Bible? What is the difference which exists between the cognitive status of the marriage question which dictates that it should be treated differently than the questions relating to the inspiration and authority of the Bible, the existence of God, and the deity of Christ?

To be perfectly fair toward Shelly, it must be admitted that he denies advancing an "agnostic epistemology" in his article "Must We Divide?,"[11] but his initial article is not the only public documentation available on this subject. Shelly is also on record as stating the following in a lecture devoted to an appeal for the restoration of the liberty of opinion:

> Here then are matters of essentials; the doctrine about Christ, who he is, what he's done for us, how he saves us, and our

response to the gospel in faith, repentance, and baptism, the church to which he adds us and how those who are members of that church are to live godly and holy and pure lives.

On the other hand there are matters of opinion, matters of conscience, matters of whether or not to observe a day as having any religious significance or not, the sabbath day, Christmas, whether or not to eat meat or to be a vegetarian. About these things we may never come to total unanimity. But that's alright. Those are matters of opinion and personal judgment and let each man be fully persuaded in his own mind, and to the Lord he stands or falls.

But I freely admit that that still leaves a class in between, of things still more difficult yet to handle. It sometimes happens that disagreements arise among brethren over issues which really can't be classified as just matters of non-essentials and matters of strictly opinion, where one can do one and the other the opposite and there's really no difference. Take for example the following list$_{12}$of questions that represents this middle...

Shelly gave essentially the same speech the following year, and it is from that printed lecture that we see the listing of those items which fall in this middle class of which he speaks: (1) the use of a missionary society to do the work of the church, (2) the use of mechanical instruments of music in worship, (3) the role of a Christian in warfare, (4) the role of women in teaching, leading in prayer, etc. in worship and in private devotionals, (5) marriage, divorce, and remarriage, (6) premillenialism, (7) the support of orphans and widows by the church, (8) church support of Bible departments in Christian colleges, (9) the "sponsoring church" arrangement, etc.[13]

With reference to each of these topics, Shelly indicates that they are neither essential (matters of faith) or non-essential (matters of opinion), yet he can still state further: "The Word of God, interpreted correctly by the rules of hermeneutics and sound reasoning, is capable of being applied to every one of these issues so as to settle it decisively."[14]

The immediately preceding statement would lead one to believe that it is possible to understand each of these areas of Bible study, but if that be the case, where, then, is the room for this suggested middle class? Though Shelly makes statements which properly represent the Biblical position concerning hermeneutics, he makes yet other comments which cause one to believe that the Bible cannot be understood as God intended. For example, note the following:

> And whereas some people deliberately wrest the scriptures unto their own destruction (II Peter 3:16b), there are many others who simply come upon passages which are hard to understand. Their problem is neither insincerity nor ignorance; it is the difficulty of the issue involved. No less than the apostle Peter admitted that some things in the epistles of Paul are "hard to be understood" (II Peter 3:16a). If Peter was taxed to understand some things in Holy Writ, we ought not be surprised that we struggle with certain texts and have difficulty arriving at unanimity regarding their meaning.
> On the fundamental issues of our faith which relate to salvation from sin and godly Christian living, the teaching of the Word of God is clear, explicit, and direct. The plan of salvation, for

example, is not only set forth in numerous straightforward statements but is also presented in several precedent-setting cases of conversion in Acts. On the other hand, several of the topics which exercise our brotherhood occasionally and threaten to disrupt fellowship are those about which far less information is available and for which there are no examples of how the earliest believers handled them.[15]

In the previous quotation Shelly mentions the following: (1) some passages are hard to understand, (2) some individuals cannot come to an understanding of certain passages, not due to insincerity or ignorance, but rather due to the difficulty of the issue, (3) Peter stated that certain things in Paul's writing were "hard to be understood," (4) Peter, therefore, was "taxed to understand some things in Holy Writ," (5) if Peter had some trouble understanding some passages, we can rest assured that we will have some difficulty as well, (6) fundamental issues regarding salvation are abundantly clear as to their meaning due to "numerous straightforward statements" and "several precedent-setting cases of conversion in Acts," and (7) those issues which cause some brethren problems are those about which "far less information is available and for which there are no examples of how the earliest believers handled them."

With regard to Shelly's comments above, some brief criticisms are in order:

(1) No one can deny that some Bible passages are not as easily understood as others. No one can maintain that the difficulty of these passages is due to a lack of sincerity. But with respect to the matter of ignorance, it must be noted that the acquisition of knowledge dispels ignorance. The more a person learns about any given subject, the less ignorant about that subject he becomes. The less ignorant one becomes about any given subject, the more likely he will

understand it.

(2) With respect to Peter's statement in II Peter 3:16, it must be noted that Peter was not advocating an agnostic position concerning the interpretation and the understanding of Scripture. He did, however, admit that some passages, specifically those written by Paul, were difficult to understand, but this did not mean that they were not subject to interpretation and understanding. Furthermore, it seems most unlikely that Peter, an inspired apostle, did not fully understand the teachings of Paul himself. The difficulty attributed to the writings of Paul, therefore, may very well have been a reference to the trouble that others had with Paul's letters.

(3) Furthermore, regarding the ease of interpretation and understanding of the Bible, it must be noted that the greater number of times a subject or doctrine is mentioned is no guarantee that it will be easily understood. Conversely, simply because a subject or doctrine is discussed relatively few times, or even one time, does not indicate that this subject is therefore extremely difficult or impossible to understand.

(4) In addition to that, it must be noted that the demand for examples in every practice will lead to even further difficulty in the interpretation and understanding of the Bible's teachings. For instance, we have no Biblical example whatsoever of an early New Testament church owning and maintaining a building for the purpose of worship and Bible study. Should such lack of example relegate the question of church buildings to a matter of Shelly's middle position? I think not.

Though specific examples of Biblical practices and doctrines are indeed helpful, they are not absolutely necessary in the interpretation and the understanding of Scripture.

Example Three

Before beginning the actual argumentation of the thesis, it will prove suitable to cite an illustration of the consequences of Shelly's agnostic position relative to the question of marriage, divorce, and remarriage.

Twice in the last few years an article has appeared in <u>UP REACH</u> magazine entitled "Throw Away Marriages." The intent of that article, as I understand it, was to teach the necessity of commitment in marriage. The lack of this distinguishing characteristic has caused many marriages to fail, and the author correctly speaks of the essentiality of this vital quality. But, within the article, the author manifested the ultimate consequences of the hermeneutical agnosticism as suggested by Shelly. In that article, we note the following remarks regarding Matthew 19:1-9 about the subject of marriage, divorce, and remarriage.

> But doesn't Jesus teach here that in cases of infidelity divorce is permitted? Yes. But He does not make divorce <u>mandatory</u> even in cases of marital unchastity.
> He said, "...whoever divorces his wife, except for unchastity, and marries another, commits adultery." This "except" clause ("except for unchastity") is the subject of controversy today, as the Deuteronomy law was among the Jews in Jesus' day.
> There are four positions taken:
> 1) Some explain the clause away entirely and insist there is <u>no</u> scriptual (sic) ground for divorce today.
> 2) Some argue that divorce is permitted, but not remarriage.
> 3) There are those who feel that adultery gives grounds for both divorce and remarriage.
> 4) Some argue there are other grounds for divorce, and perhaps remarriage,

besides adultery. For instance, these may point to the desertion of a Christian by a non-Christian (cf. 1 Corinthians 7:15).[16]

Due to my concern for the issues involved, I wrote to inquire about the article.

In private correspondence with one of the elders of the congregation that oversees the publication of UP REACH magazine, I questioned the inclusion of Mr. Barnett's statement. I set forth my question in the following way:

> Does the eldership of the Highland church of Christ agree with the manner in which Joe Barnett discussed the subject of marriage and divorce and remarriage in the May/June 1980 issue of UP REACH in which brother Barnett listed four positions taken with regard to the subject, but which he did not say were either correct or incorrect? (What would you think if I wrote an article about the subject of baptism and said that there were four positions about it: 1) it is unnecessary, 2) it is unnecessary for salvation, but necessary to join the church, 3) it is necessary but can be by sprinkling, and 4) it is necessary but can only be by immersion. If I never mentioned which ones were right or wrong, would you agree with the article?)[17]

In response to that letter, I received a reply from the same elder of the Highland church of Christ in Abilene, Texas, which said in part:

> Number four—marriage—There is much controversy over marriage, divorce, and remarriage in the Lord's church today all across the brotherhood. It seems a

healthy situation to let people know some of the approaches being made on the divorce and remarriage problem. I would say that Joe Barnett believes much as you do.[18]

The elder made no response to my question about the hypothetical article I suggested regarding the four positions on baptism. Instead, he responded to the question about Barnett's article by saying that "it seems a healthy situation to let people know some of the approaches being made on the divorce and remarriage problem." **But which ones are right? Which ones are wrong? Are they all right? Are they all wrong?**

To respond by saying that controversy exists about the question is not much of a response at all. To state that the author "believes much as you do" is somewhat evasive, to say the very least. I made no comments whatsoever relative to which positions about the question I endorsed, or which I held to be false. Should this sort of approach to any Bible topic be considered, we would not claim to know anything. This might occur because we really did not know anything about the Bible other than lists of possibilities, or it might occur only on those subjects which are "controversial," in order to placate opposing parties.

It is the contention of this writer that the controversial nature or the degree of difficulty of any Bible subject does not necessarily relegate the cognitive status of that subject to something less than those subjects we consider easy and obvious to understand. To rely upon the difficult nature of any subject as an escape only tends to promote an agnostic position.

Conclusion

In the previous example cited (i.e., example two), we noted that Shelly argued for a specific position, and therefore does not endorse any position in opposition to his.

But, what does the endorsement of any given position amount to if the person who gives it is not absolutely and positively sure of the correctness of it? To state that one's "intellective powers are not infallible" when suggested as a constant gauge against which every intellectually held position must be measured and found wanting, is simply to say that that person **does not know** and **cannot know** if his position (with regard to which the statement was first made) is correct. It makes no difference whether or not his position is really correct. If he is not sure about it, he certainly cannot claim to know the truthfulness of his position. Antony G.N. Flew stated this principle as follows:

> Abraham Lincoln was profoundly right when he wrote, chiding the editor of a Springfield newspaper: 'It is an established maxim and moral that he who makes an assertion without knowing whether it is true or false is guilty of a falsehood, and the accidental truth of the assertion does not justify or excuse him.' It is also true that to tolerate contradiction is similarly to be indifferent to truth. For the person who, whether directly or by implication, knowingly both asserts and denies one and the same proposition, shows by that behaviour that he does not care whether he asserts what is false, and not true, or whether he denies what is true, and not false.[19]

Knowledge, if it takes three seconds or even thirty years to attain, is still knowledge. The degree of difficulty encountered in the attainment of that knowledge (Biblical or otherwise) does not change the cognitive status of the information acquired.

Everything is either (1) **knowable, and thus either known or unknown** or (2) **unknowable and thus unknown.** To create a "class in between" that which is knowable and that which is unknowable is but to refuse to admit the law of excluded middle and so catapult oneself headlong into agnosticism.

The dangers of advocating agnosticism, especially under the guise of intellectual humility (e.g., "my intellective powers are not infallible") is most dangerous indeed. Tom Eddins notes the following with regard to this point:

> In many ways agnosticism is "in." It is supposed by many to exhibit an intellectual humility that should characterize any Christian scholar. What is supposed to be the opposite extreme (i.e. "dogmatism") is abhorred, and those making a claim to absolute knowledge (in almost any area) are usually branded as arrogant, bigots, etc. One author has written, "We are on the road to producing a race of men too mentally modest to believe in the multiplication table."[20]

---

1. There will, no doubt, be those who strongly disagree with this writer's assessment of the following instances as exemplifying an agnostic stance, but, given the specific wording of the examples cited, no other reasonable conclusion could be drawn.

2. Joe Beam, "I Know I'm Right!", FIRM FOUNDATION, ed. by Reuel Lemmons, May 12, 1981, p. 291

3. This argument assumes the supreme authority and integrity of Christ, and the truthfulness of the Bible's record of Christ's statements. Subsequent arguments will demonstrate that the Bible is the word of God,

thus assuring us that all statements by Christ are true.

4. Maintaining an agnostic position with respect to a single Bible subject is not at all dangerous if that subject is actually beyond human cognition. If, however, the subject is "knowable" (or even **must** be known), then **it is dangerous** to maintain an agnostic position.

5. Shelly, in a later article, denies that this first article promulgates an agnostic stance. With all due respect to Shelly, this writer must politely disagree. The explicit statements of the article under consideration warrant the comments expressed herein.

6. Rubel Shelly, "Must We Divide?," FIRM FOUNDATION, ed. by Reuel Lemmons, January 6, 1981, p. 8

7. This argumentation draws upon material supplied in Thomas B. Warren, Keeping The Lock In Wedlock (Jonesboro, Ark.: National Christian Press, 1980), p. 10ff

8. For further information concerning the specifics of the Bible's teaching on marriage, divorce, and remarriage, see Warren's book and the subsequent chapters of this work.

9. Rubel Shelly, What Shall We Do With The Bible? (Jonesboro, Ark.: National Christian Press, 1975), p. ix

10. Ibid., p. x

11. cf. Rubel Shelly, "Follow Up Thoughts On 'Must We Divide?'", FIRM FOUNDATION, ed. by Reuel Lemmons, December 15, 1981, p. 792

12. Rubel Shelly, "The Restoration Of The Liberty Of Opinion," taped lecture given at David Lipscomb

College, June 16, 1981 Note: Due to the end of side one of the tape, Shelly's speech was interrupted.

13. Rubel Shelly, "Christ, The Effective Energy For Unity In The Brotherhood," in <u>Christ Our Effective Energy—Eighth Annual Lectureship</u> (Knoxville, Tn.: East Tennessee School Of Preaching And Missions, 1982), pp. 147-148

14. Ibid., 148

15. Ibid., pp. 148-149

16. Joe R. Barnett, "Throw Away Marriages," in UP REACH, ed. by Batsell Barrett Baxter, May/June 1980, p. 19 and March/April 1981, p. 7

17. private letter sent to an elder of the Highland church of Christ, April 11, 1981, by author.

18. private letter sent by an elder of the Highland church of Christ, May 6, 1981, to author.

19. Antony G.N. Flew, <u>Thinking Straight</u> (Buffalo, N.Y.: Prometheus Books, 1975), p. 15

20. Tom Eddins, "Can We Really Be Certain?," SPIRITUAL SWORD, ed. by Thomas B. Warren, July 1977, p. 23 The author cited by Eddins is G.K. Chesterton, quoted in J.R.W. Stott, <u>Christ The Controversialist</u> (Downers Grove, Ill.: Inter-Varsity Press, 1970), pp. 15-16

CHAPTER NINE-A:

ARGUMENTATION AGAINST AGNOSTICISM

This section of the work, along with the following chapter, constitutes the most important part of this endeavor.

In this section it will be the writer's purpose to accomplish the following: (1) to explain the necessity of hermeneutics, (2) to present argumentation against agnosticism in general, (3) to present argumentation against agnosticism as it relates to Biblical interpretation, and (4) to prepare the way for positive argumentation of the thesis to take place in chapter ten.

The argumentation in this chapter will show the weaknesses of agnosticism in general, and hermeneutical agnosticism in particular. The argumentation in the subsequent chapter will present several positive arguments, each of which will yield as their concluding premise the basic thesis of this paper, that is, that we can know that the Bible teaches X where X represents any true Bible proposition which is subject to human cognition.

The Necessity Of Hermeneutics

In the opening paragraph of chapter four it was noted that most of the written works devoted to a discussion of the subject of Biblical interpretation concern themselves with a listing, exposition, and explanation of certain rules and methods of hermeneutics. Though this information and style of approach is important, very few deal with the fundamental question in hermeneutics: can we **KNOW** that the Bible can be understood? Most works simply assume that such is possible, and though this assumption is correct (as will be demonstrated by this work), they never set forth the case to **PROVE**, in a demonstrative way, that this assumption is correct.

There exists, however, an equally fundamental aspect of Biblical interpretation that is also overlooked. We must, in addition to understanding that Biblical hermeneutics is possible, also understand that hermeneutics is **necessary**. Indeed, in a very real sense, understanding the necessity of hermeneutics is logically prior to understanding that hermeneutics is possible. An explanation is in order.

Many people have the idea that the Bible is, or should be, like any other popular and contemporary literature that one might pick up to read. This, however, is not quite what we find.

As we read newspapers, magazines, professional periodicals, briefs, novels, and even science fiction thrillers, we are reading materials with which we have a great deal of familiarity. We do not, however, usually have anywhere near that same sort or degree of familiarity with the Bible.

That lack of familiarity with the background of the Bible is not so unnatural. The Bible was written during a period beginning 1500 years before the birth of Christ and ending approximately 70 years after his death, a total of almost 1600 years.

It was written in languages different than our own. It was written by men of different backgrounds during times that were different historically, politically, religiously, socially, ethically, and so forth. They lived in different parts of the world where different customs and ideas were part of their culture, but certainly not part of ours today. Their languages were replete with words, phrases, and idioms foreign to our own.[1]

It is no great wonder then, that the Bible needs to be understood in light of all of these differences, which account for the lack of ease with which people approach Bible study. The Bible, because of its great differences in background, does not seem "real" to the average person. The daily newspapers, weekly magazines, and contemporary novels are real to us only because of our proximity to them. It is essential, therefore, to understand that the magnitude of the Bible's differences in background necessitate Biblical interpretation.

The Bible is not, however, so unusual that it occupies a class all by itself when it comes to interpretation. There exist numerous other works which must be understood through the same process of interpretation. A. Berkeley Mickelsen points this out when he says:

> The need for interpretation is not peculiar to the Scriptures. Any document, ancient or modern, must be interpreted. The decisions of the Supreme Court are actually interpretations of the Constitution of the United States. Philosophers often debate what Plato, Aristotle, or Kant meant by certain phrases or assertions. The archaeologist who carefully analyzes a religious writing from the Dead Sea Scrolls often finds statements that puzzle him, and he must use all the principles and skills he knows to reach even a tentative conclusion of meaning.[2]

Rene Marle emphasizes the same thought when he states the following:

> It was not, therefore, left to Christianity to invent the problem of hermeneutics, at least in its specifically theological context; it was already well known in Greek antiquity, when the hermeneutists were preoccupied with ascertaining the meaning of the myths that had been transmitted; and in general, the meaning of the poetical works, especially the Homeric writings. An entire division of culture, so to speak, was

dedicated to the interpretation of these fundamental data, namely, the trilogy of grammar, rhetoric, and poetics. Aristotle in particular was concerned with establishing their laws. Along with the effort to master the pure techniques of language, moreover, which would allow for a true grasp of the literal meaning of a text, there also arose an effort at interpretation which sought to attain a more profound, interpretative understanding of the same text;...[3]

J.W. Roberts, like the previous writers (Mickelsen and Marle), also emphasized that the need to interpret the Bible was most natural, not because of its relation to other works which also demonstrated the need for interpretation, but because of the nature of writing in general.

We need not hesitate in the admission that the Bible must be interpreted. Of course the Bible means "just what it says." But "what it says" involves who said it, to whom it was said, under what circumstance it was said, and whether it was directly by way of commandment or indirectly by example or inference. It also involves what is left unsaid and what (for reasons of silence) is a matter of indifference or expediency and what (for other reasons of silence) is excluded.[4]

The objective of hermeneutics, both Biblical and secular, therefore, is to ascertain the intended meaning of the text under consideration. Mickelsen says: "Simply stated, the task of interpreters of the Bible is <u>to find out the meaning of a statement (command, question) for the author and for the first hearers or readers, and thereupon to transmit that meaning to</u>

modern readers."[5]

The necessity of hermeneutics, then, is evidenced by all Bible scholars.

It must be pointed out, however, that the necessity of hermeneutics does not guarantee that the methods and principles of interpretation employed will yield the original intent of the author. Numerous interpretations of passages have been developed by different scholars, all of whom understand the necessity of hermeneutics. The different interpretations arose, not because each understood that interpretation was necessary, but rather because each applied the same hermeneutical principle in different ways, or because altogether different hermeneutical principles were applied.

Hermeneutics, then, though necessary, must be properly applied. The problem with the religious world, as Alexander Campbell has said, is due in great part to the application of "false principles of interpretation, or by a misapplication of true principles."[6]

If it were the case that all those who believed in the Bible as the inspired word of God also interpreted the Bible in the same manner and came up with the same conclusions, then the religious differences which exist in the world, to which Campbell alluded, would almost dissipate entirely, thus resulting in the greater likelihood of the conversion of unbelievers. Lamar, in his book <u>The Organon Of Scripture</u>, contends earnestly toward that end.

> The great voice which rises up from this mass of doubting, hesitating, unbelieving mind is, "Point out the truth, and we will receive it; tell us what the Scriptures <u>mean</u>, and we will follow them; but amid the thousand discords and clamorous strifes, the antagonistic doctrines and discrepant interpretations, we cannot determine what to believe or what to do." And thus infidelity—routed from the ground it once so proudly and

- 67 -

defiantly occupied, and compelled to relinquish into the hands of the Church its hold upon science, criticism, and history, with which at one time it threatened the overthrow of the truth—has taken refuge in a <u>fortress built by the Church</u>. Our divisions, contentions, and differences have given birth to, and builded the stronghold of a skepticism the most pernicious and insinuating, which prevails as widely as Christendom; which is giving life and support to all manner of false religions; a skepticism which often sits at the communion table of the Lord; which grows up with our religious education, and is confirmed by the weekly preaching from our pulpits; and which the Church can never reach till she becomes able to destroy her own work.[7]

It is most apparent, then, that Bible scholars admit the necessity of Biblical hermeneutics. This is not by any means our sole source of authority, for **the Bible itself teaches the necessity of hermeneutics, and encourages the student of the word of God to make proper application of those principles.**

Perhaps the most frequently cited passage which demonstrates this need is II Timothy 2:15. It says: "Study to show thyself approved unto God, a workman that needeth not to be ashamed, rightly dividing the word of truth."

The term "rightly dividing" comes from the Greek word **orthotomeo**, the meaning of which is the single most important factor in this verse as it relates to hermeneutics. Its meaning has confused many, lead others to establish myriads of topical and chronological divisions, and prompted numerous sermons on the necessity of studying the word of God.[8]

All of these are well and good, but in light of the general tenor of Paul's epistles to Timothy, and especially in view of the immediate context, it seems that Paul is emphasizing the need for Timothy to "rightly divide" ("handling aright", ASV) the word of truth by PRACTICING its precepts in his own life.[9] This thought is reflected by Helmut Koster in his comments concerning the meaning of the term.

In the one NT instance of **orthotomeo** (2Tm.2:15) the figurative idea of the way is so pale that a theological concept can be the direct object: **orthotomounta ton logon tes aletheias,** cf. Herm.v., 3, 5, 3 ... Whereas the false teachers engage in irreligious theological chatter which can only destroy their hearers and which leads to an ungodly walk (2:14, 16), Timothy is to be a workman of God who need not be ashamed since he "does what is right with reference to the word of truth." This cannot mean in the context that Timothy should "trim" or "handle" the word of truth rightly. The view that he is to deliver the word of truth correctly in proclamation is also impossible in view of the parallels adduced. One can no longer take into account the metaphorical aspect, nor can the word of truth be the object of Timothy's **orthotomeo** in the simple sense. Rather one is to construe the expression along the line of **katorthoomai tas entolas** (Herm. v., 3, 5, 3) and **orthopodeo pros ten aletheian tou euangeliou** (Gl.2:14 > V, 451, 16 ff.). In his conduct Timothy must "speak the word of truth aright," i.e., follow it. When he puts his acts under the word of truth he is worthy before God and need not be ashamed, 2 Tm.2:15. He is superior to the false teachers, not because he can present the word better, nor because he offers it in a theologically legitimate form, but because he follows the word of truth aright in his own life, and thus confirms it.[70]

The emphasis, rightly made by Koster, is that the term has primary reference to the **application** (i.e., practice) of godly principles to Timothy's life. This would, of course, not only **include** understanding what the Bible teaches, but it would also of necessity **demand understanding** what the Bible teaches.

It is **impossible** to put into practice what one does not understand. We are to understand the comments of John (Revelation 1:3) in exactly the same way. In that passage John says: "Blessed is he that readeth, and they that hear the words of this prophecy, and keep those things which are written therein: for the time is at hand."

Notice the conditions upon which blessings come: (1) reading, (2) hearing, and (3) keeping the things which are written. It is **impossible** to "keep" (i.e., follow, obey) that which one does not understand. This passage, then, like II Timothy 2:15, tacitly affirms that the Bible can be understood. **As a matter of fact, every Bible passage which demands obedience, of any sort, also demands that that passage can be understood, as well as followed.**

Furthermore, in Acts 8:26-40, we note the account of the conversion of the Ethiopian eunuch, which also informs us of the necessity of proper interpretation. In that account we note that the eunuch was reading from a passage of Scripture that we now know as Isaiah 53:7-8. With respect to his understanding of that passage we note the following:

> And he arose and went: and behold, a man of Ethiopia, a eunuch of great authority under Candace queen of the Ethiopians, who had the charge of all her treasure, and had come to Jerusalem for

> to worship, was returning, and sitting in his chariot read Isaiah the prophet. Then the Spirit said unto Philip, Go near, and join thyself to this chariot. And Philip ran thither to him, and heard him read the prophet Isaiah, and said, Understandest thou what thou readest? And he said, How can I, except some man should guide me? And he desired Philip that he would come up and sit with him.

As the passage continues, we note that Philip taught the eunuch the intended meaning and application of that passage from the book of Isaiah by properly teaching the eunuch about the Christ.

In order to teach the truth with respect to this or any other Bible passage, it was necessary for Philip to properly interpret the passage under consideration. Though Philip, as an inspired evangelist, may have been speaking through the influence of the Holy Spirit, the principle remains the same. All Christians today are to teach the lost, as did Philip. We do not, however, have the miraculous power of the Holy Spirit. We must, therefore, in order to fulfill the Lord's command, understand the necessity of hermeneutics, as well as have the ability to implement hermeneutics.

It is only too self-evident that a failure to properly interpret any given Bible passage will yield a faulty conclusion and perhaps a faulty application as well. That Philip taught the eunuch correctly is tantamount to saying that he interpreted the Scripture correctly. Rather than saying "How can I, except some man should guide me," the eunuch could very well have said: "How can I except that some man should interpret the passage for me?"

Many more Bible passages could be cited in demonstration of the necessity of proper interpretation, but these will suffice for the present discussion.

We have noted, therefore, that Biblical interpretation is absolutely necessary if we are to understand the intended meaning of the writers, who wrote, of course, through the inspiration of the Holy Spirit of God. Their words, then, were not just of human origin, but also of divine origin and influence (II Peter 1:19-21).

In addition to that, we have noted that interpretation is applied to areas other than religion. It is used in the areas of archaeology, classical literature, and law, just to mention a few.

The objective of hermeneutics in each of these areas is to ascertain the initial meaning of the author/speaker and thus the intended understanding of the immediate audience. Ideally, the understanding of the audience will be identical to the initial intent of the author, but sometimes this is not the case.

For example, the apostle Paul mentioned several things concerning the coming of Christ and the status of the dead in his first epistle to the church at Thessalonica which he later had to re-explain in his next epistle. This was evidently due to a misunderstanding on the part of the Thessalonians of the contents of Paul's first letter. The point is, however, that **we must strive to attain God's intended meaning of Scripture.**

General Arguments

As previously noted, "agnosticism" as first used by T.H. Huxley had primary reference to the question of God's existence. In addition to that, it has been further explained that the connotation of the term has been expanded to cover other objects of human inquiry.

It becomes necessary, therefore, to defend the basic thesis of this work against the **general** theory of agnosticism.

Agnosticism, strictly speaking, is an epistemological theory which states that certain elements can not be subject to cognition due either to the nature of those elements or due to man's limited ability to know those elements as true or false.

Though it is the burden of this thesis to disprove agnosticism as a general epistemological theory, it must be admitted that there are certain objects of thought, which to a degree, will forever remain beyond the scope of human understanding. It is indeed conceivable that one might properly maintain an "agnostic" position with regard to some particulars without adopting the basic epistemological approach called "agnosticism." In much the same way, the gospel of Christ is pragmatic, yet it is not philosophical "pragmatism."

Thus, a person might remain agnostic with regard to the right answers to the following questions: (1) Can we completely understand the incarnation of Christ? No, we cannot. (2) Can we know completely the mind/body relationship? No, we cannot. (3) Can we know all there is to know about the Holy Spirit's relationship to the Christian? No, we cannot. (4) Can we know whether or not God will create an additional "world" for his pleasure following the destruction of this present world? No, we cannot.

With reference to the above questions, it can be truly said that all we can have, epistemologically speaking, is an agnostic position. These elements are simply beyond the limits of human cognitive ability. No harm is thereby done when we use the term "agnostic" as correctly descriptive of the human mental position with regard to the answers to these questions and others like them.

We must further differentiate between knowledge as it varies from individual to individual. It is possible for a man to lack knowledge with respect to a certain proposition. That lack of knowledge, however, does not warrant the conclusion that this specific proposition is not subject to cognition by any one else, and thus an agnostic position. It may be possible for another man to have an understanding with reference to the very same proposition about which the first man had no knowledge. Furthermore, due to limited physical and mental ability, a certain individual may not be able to fathom a given proposition to any extent whatsoever. To that individual, the specific proposition lies beyond his real limits. On the other hand, that proposition may be very well understood by an average person not beset with any mental or physical handicaps. In such an instance, it may be the case that the term agnostic can be correctly applied to one person, but not to another.

To sum up, a thing may not be known because: (1) it is not knowable even by God (e.g., logical contradictions such as "square circles," "round triangles"), (2) it is knowable by God, but not accessible to man (cf. Deuteronomy 29:29), (3) it is accessible to man, but has not been mentally approached, and (4) it is accessible to man, but can only be attained through strenuous mental application, an attempt at which has not been made.

Concerning this work, however, the term agnostic and/or agnosticism, will be understood to refer to that which is beyond the cognitive ability of **all** men. To make a claim that one must occupy an agnostic position relative to a certain question or proposition, therefore, is to claim that such a proposition is beyond the cognizance of any human being. It is, perhaps, that which might be termed "objective agnosticism."

To make such a claim with respect to those enterprises which are in reality beyond the limits of human reflection is not to commit any epistemological blunder, but to affirm that a certain enterprise is beyond human understanding, when it is in reality actually subject to human knowledge, is most assuredly a misapplication of the term agnosticism.

It is this last instance, the misapplication of the term agnosticism, that this work proposes to refute. It is not the goal of this section to prove that all agnosticism is wrong, for such is incapable of proof. As previously mentioned, there are legitimate occasions in which the use of the term agnosticism is warranted. Instead, it will be the immediate goal of this section to show the fallacy of espousing an agnostic stance with reference to those elements and propositions which are in reality subject to human understanding.

Taken to its furthest application, agnosticism denies the possibility of any knowledge, regardless of the discipline under consideration. This radical approach, however, is subject to rejection due to the logical contradictions involved in attempting to maintain this position.

Note first the argument for agnosticism (A = agnosticism is a true epistemological position, K = man has the ability to know):

(1) A > -K (definitional)
(2) A (assumed by agnostics)
(3) -K (1,2 Modus Ponens)

In ordinary language, the gist of the argument for agnosticism might be given as follows: (1) If agnosticism is a true epistemological position, then man does not have the ability to know. (2) Agnosticism is a true epistemological position. (3) Therefore man does not have the ability to know.

This argument is valid in form, but due to a false premise (i.e., premise two), the argument is definitely not a sound one. In addition to this, it must be mentioned that the proponent of this argument must be responsible for providing proof for the truthfulness of the second premise, for it is that premise which is the most crucial in the argument. If it can really be proven true, then the argument is not only valid, but also sound, and the conclusion, "man does not have the ability to know," would be true.

In like manner, the following argument could be given in defense of agnosticism (using the same symbols):

(1) -K > A (see discussion to follow)
(2) -K (assumed by agnostics)
(3) A (1, 2 Modus Ponens)

This argument would read as follows: (1) If man does not have the ability to know, then agnosticism is a true epistemological position. (2) Man does not have the ability to know. (3) Therefore agnosticism is a true epistemological position.

The difference between this argument and the previous one begins in the first premise. In the previous argument, the first premise was A > -K (If agnosticism is a true epistemological position, then man does not have the ability to know.). The first premise of the second argument is -K > A (If man does not have the ability to know, then agnosticism is a true epistemological position.). Both of these premises are true definitionally. That is to say that the antecedent and the consequent are related, as a term and a definition of that term are related. In the second argument, like the first, the second premise is the key premise. Agnostics must prove that man does not have the ability to know.

The absurdity of such argumentation is seen to be evident in the contradictions which agnosticism entails. Notice the following closely related arguments which pitch agnosticism into defeat (using the same symbols):

Argument #1

(1) (A > -K) > K (see discussion below)
(2) -K (assumed by agnostics)
(3) -(A > -K) (1, 2 Modus Tollens)

Argument #2

(1) -K > -(A > -K) (arg.1, prem.1-transposition)
(2) -K (assumed by agnostics)
(3) -(A > -K) (1, 2 Modus Ponens)

The arguments would read as follows:

Argument#1—(1) If it is the case that agnosticism implies that man does not have the ability to know, then in order to maintain that premise, one must have knowledge. (2) But agnosticism affirms that man cannot know. (3) Therefore, it is false to affirm that agnosticism implies that man cannot know. Argument #2—(1) If man does not have the ability to know, then it is false to affirm that agnostics can know that man cannot know. (2) Agnosticism affirms that man cannot know. (3) Therefore, it is false to affirm that agnosticism implies that man cannot know.

In the first argument cited above, the following details must be pointed out. The first premise of that argument [(A > -K) > K] is the first premise of the basic argument cited previously in defense of agnosticism, with one important exception. That exception is, of course, that that premise [(A > -K)] is shown here as it implies that knowledge is actually possible. It would read as follows: If it is true that agnosticism implies that man cannot come to knowledge (the agnostic's claim), then it is true this this claim implies knowledge [i.e., that one can know the truthfulness of the premise (A > -K)].

The second premise of the first argument (-K) is the conclusion of the basic argument for agnosticism, which simply states that man cannot come to knowledge. But, if that premise is true, and assuming the agnostic is correct in asserting that it is true, then he is thrown into the midst of a quandary.

If the second premise is true, and we shall grant that it is for the sake of this argument, then the conclusion which follows via the logical move of Modus Tollens renders the antecedent of the first premise [(A > -K)] as false. The force of this argument quite simply shows that the agnostic's basic argument is, in and of itself, a claim to knowledge, which claim the agnostic initially sought to deny. **Such a contradiction could not be more telling.**

Furthermore, we note in the second argument that the same conclusion [(A > -K)] can be reached through an argument in the form of Modus Ponens. In this argument the first premise is logically equivalent to the first premise of argument number one. When the logical move "transposition" is applied to that premise (i.e., premise one of argument one), then it yields premise one of argument number two.[11]

The first premise simply states that if it is not possible for man to know, then the agnostic can not know that his position implies that we cannot know. This is axiomatic. If knowledge is not possible, an agnostic (or anyone else for that matter) cannot know anything.

In the second argument, as with the first, the second premise (-K) is the conclusion which the agnostic assumes in his basic argument, namely that man does not have the ability to know. Though it is a false conclusion, the truthfulness of it is assumed for the purpose of this argument. When that premise is assumed to be true, it constitutes proof of the antecedent of premise one, and through the logical move known as Modus Ponens, it yields the conclusion that the consequent [-(A > -K)] is true (i.e., if the premises are true).

The second argument, then, reaches the same conclusion as does the first: **The agnostic cannot know that his conclusion that knowledge is not attainable is true. Thus, he cannot know that the affirmation of agnosticism is true.**

But agnosticism is involved in an even more telling dilemma. In addition to being false, it is logically contradictory as well. Note the following argumentation (using the same symbols):

Argument #3

(1) -K > -(A > -K) (prem. 1 of arg.2)
(2) -K > -(-A v -K) (1 Implication)
(3) -K > (A . K) (2 DeMorgan's Theorem)
(4) -K (assumed by agnostics)

(5) (A . K) (3, 4 Modus Ponens)
(6) K (5 Simplification)
(7) (K . -K) (4, 6 Conjunction)

The argument reads as follows: (1) If man does not have the ability to know, then man cannot know that agnosticism implies that man cannot know. (2) If man does not have the ability to know, then man cannot know that either agnosticism is false or it is not possible for man to know. (3) If man does not have the ability to know, then agnosticism is true and the proposition "man does have the ability to know" is true. (4) Man does not have the ability to know. (This is the agnostic assumption made for the purposes of this argument.) (5) Agnosticism is a true epistemological position and man has the ability to know. (6) Man has the ability to know. (7) Man has the ability to know and man does not have the ability to know.

In the preceding argument, when the conclusion of agnosticism is assumed to be true (i.e., premise 4, -K), the argument results in a logical contradiction (K . -K). Because one cannot maintain the truthfulness of any given proposition when it implies the "truthfulness" of a logical contradiction, it is obvious that that which implies a logical contradiction is false.

Agnosticism, because it implies that one can know and not know at the same time, is guilty of a logical contradiction. Agnosticism, therefore, is seen to be false in its basic approach to epistemology.

With reference to this self-defeating tendency inherent in agnosticism, note the following:

> When one affirms the proposition "No one can know anything" he has both affirmed and denied the same thing. This is true because he is claiming to know that no one can know. Obviously, this is self-contradictory. No one can rationally claim that no one can know anything.

And yet, this is the very thing that agnostics attempt to do.[12]

That no one can rationally maintain an agnostic position with reference to epistemology is further borne out by the same author when he states:

> ...if agnosticism is the correct epistemological approach, according to it no one could know that it is the correct approach. Thus, it would be absolutely a waste of time in attempting to persuade others of its correctness, for no one could know that it is correct. If one could come to know of the correctness of the agnostic approach, he would be knowing something. But this is the very thing that agnosticism denies.[13]

Generally speaking, then, agnosticism is an untenable approach. It is untenable because it is self-defeating. It is untenable because it is self-contradictory. It is untenable because it is not subject to logical demonstration, but rather subject to disproof. Quite simply stated, if it is possible for man to know something (anything), then it is false that agnosticism is true. It is possible for a man to know something (anything). Therefore, it is false that agnosticism is true.

Stated in symbolic form (using the same symbols), it would appear as follows:

(1) K > -A
(2) K
(3) -A (1, 2 Modus Ponens)

The argument could also be rephrased as follows: If agnosticism is true, then man cannot know. But man can know, therefore agnosticism cannot be true. It would appear as:

(1) A > -K
(2) K
(3) -A (1, 2 Modus Tollens)

In both of the above arguments the crucial premise is the second one. As proof of premise two, one need only demonstrate that he knows 2 + 2 = 4 or that he knows his own name. Having done so, the conclusion, by Modus Ponens (the first argument) or Modus Tollens (the second argument), follows. **Agnosticism is, therefore, a false epistemological view.**

---

1. cf. Robert Milligan, Reason And Revelation (Cincinnati, Ohio: R.W. Carroll and Company, Publishers, 1868, reprinted by Lambert Book House 1975), p. 287ff

2. A. Berkeley Mickelsen, Interpreting The Bible (Grand Rapids: William B. Eerdmans Publishing Company, 1963), p. 3

3. Rene Marle, Introduction To Hermeneutics (New York: Herder and Herder, 1967), p. 12

4. J.W. Roberts, "Expediency And Pattern Authority," in Abilene Christian College Lectures-1960 (Abilene, TX.: Abilene Christian College, 1960), p. 382

5. Mickelsen, Interpreting The Bible, p. 5

6. Alexander Campbell, Christianity Restored: "The Principle Extras Of The Millennial Harbinger, Revised And Corrected" (Rosemead, Ca.: The Old Paths Book Club, 1959), p. 15

7. Lamar, The Organon Of Scripture, pp. 22-23

8. cf. M.R. Vincent, <u>Word Studies In The New Testament-Vol. II</u> (McLean, Va.: MacDonald Publishing Company, n.d.), p. 1059

9. The term **orthotomeo** is also used in the Septuagint (Proverbs 3:6; 11:5) in the context of discussing "right living."

10. Helmut Koster, "**ORTHOTOMEO**," in <u>Theological Dictionary Of The New Testament-Vol. VIII</u> ed. by Gerhard Kittel, Gerhard Friedrich (Grand Rapids: William B. Eerdmans Publishing Company, 1972), p. 112

11. cf. Copi, <u>Introduction To Logic</u>, p. 319 for further information about "transposition."

12. Mac Deaver, "Agnosticism Is Self-Defeating," SPIRITUAL SWORD, ed. by Thomas B. Warren, July 1977, p. 14

13. Ibid., p. 15

CHAPTER NINE-B:

ARGUMENTATION AGAINST AGNOSTICISM

The previous section of this chapter dealt with argumentation against agnosticism from a **general perspective.** This section will deal with agnosticism from a **specific point of view,** that of the realm of **Biblical interpretation.** It will be the purpose of this section to present **argumentation** which yields the conclusion that agnosticism, as it relates to hermeneutics, is a **false epistemological position.** Positive argumentation in defense of the specific thesis will be presented in chapter ten.

Four arguments will be presented in these two sections (chapters 9-B and 9-C). Each of those four arguments will yield as their conclusion the proposition that agnosticism in Biblical interpretation is a **false epistemological position.**

The first two arguments are very much related in that they deal with one of the many **implications** of agnosticism, namely **subjectivism.** The last two arguments are similar in that they deal with specific Bible subjects which cannot be known as either true or false if agnosticism were true. To demonstrate, therefore, that these elements of Bible teaching are, in reality **subject to cognition** (and true), is to prove that the agnostic approach to Biblical interpretation is **wrong.**

Each of the arguments will be presented first in symbolic logic form. A discussion of each argument, including discussion and proofs of the various premises, will follow the symbolic argumentation.

Specific Arguments Against Agnosticism

The first argument, presented below in symbolic terms (A = agnosticism is a true epistemological position in Biblical interpretation, S = subjectivism, X = any Bible proposition), is as follows:

Argument #1

(1) A > S (see discussion to follow)
(2) S > (X . -X) (definitional)
(3) -(X . -X) (law of non-contradiction)
(4) -S (2,3 Modus Tollens)
(5) -A (1,4 Modus Tollens)

The argumentation reads as follows: (1) If it is the case that agnosticism in Biblical interpretation is the correct and proper epistemological position, then it follows that subjectivism in Biblical interpretation will result.
(2) If subjectivism in Biblical interpretation is practiced, then it is entirely possible for one party to affirm a specific Bible proposition at the same time another party denies the same proposition, and both parties be equally right epistemologically.
(3) It is not possible for both parties, one affirming and the other denying the same proposition, to be correct.
(4) Therefore subjectivism in Biblical interpretation is a false epistemological position. If subjectivism in Biblical interpretation is false, then (5) agnosticism, as an epistemological position in Biblical interpretation, is false because it implies subjectivism.

The above argumentation is completely valid in its form. Furthermore, all of the propositions functioning as premises are true. The argument, therefore, is a sound one, and the conclusion necessarily follows.

To further elucidate the meaning of the above argument, it is necessary to demonstrate the logical consequence of affirming a logical contradiction.[1] Note the following argument presented in symbolic terms [S = subjectivism, X = any Bible proposition, or simply any proposition. Y = any other Bible proposition (not X), or simply any other proposition (not X)]:

(1) S > (X . -X) (definitional)
(2) S (assumed by agnostics)
(3) (X . -X) (1,2 Modus Ponens)
(4) X (3 Simplification)
(5) -X (3 Simplification)
(6) (X v Y) (4 Addition)
(7) Y (6,5 Disjunctive Syllogism)
(8) (X v -Y) (4 Addition)
(9) -Y (8,5 Disjunctive Syllogism)
(10) (Y . -Y) (7,9 Conjunction)

The point of this argument is really quite simple. If subjectivism implies that a given proposition (e.g., X) can be both true and false within the same frame of reference (which it does), then ultimately, any other proposition (e.g., Y) can also be both true and false within the same frame of reference. If one logical contradiction is granted, then it is logically impossible to keep from granting any and all logical contradictions as true.

It is evident from the above argument, that an effort to affirm a logical contradiction must consider that the implications of that affirmation are far reaching. If a logical contradiction is affirmed, then it is possible, based on the affirmation of that contradiction, to **both affirm and deny any other proposition.** Such demonstrates the disastrous consequences of affirming a logical contradiction.[2]

The purpose of showing the consequences of subjectivism is clear. If hermeneutical agnosticism implies subjectivism (and it does), and if subjectivism implies a logical contradiction (and it does), then agnosticism implies a logical contradiction. This was emphasized in the previous section, but worth repeating here. **Subjectivism, because it implies a logical contradiction, is false, because any logical contradiction is false. Agnosticism, therefore, because it implies subjectivism, which implies a logical contradiction, is** also false.

The second argument, as previously mentioned, is very similar to the first. This similarity is based upon further argumentation relating to subjectivism as an implication of an agnostic epistemological stance in the realm of hermeneutics. The second argument, in symbolic terms (A = agnosticism is a proper epistemological position in Biblical interpretation, S = subjectivism in Biblical interpretation is a true position, X = any Bible proposition, Z = any Bible proposition and its denial must be considered as true, KBTX = we can know the truth of the Bible's propositional statements, that is to say that we can know that the Bible teaches X, where X is any true Bible proposition), is given below:

Argument #2

(1) A > S (definitional, cf. previous arg.)
(2) S > (X . -X) (definitional, cf. previous arg.)
(3) (X . -X) > Z (obvious, cf. discussion)
(4) Z > -KBTX (obvious, cf. discussion)
(5) KBTX (proof in following section)
(6) -Z (4, 5 Modus Tollens)
(7) -(X . -X) (3, 6 Modus Tollens)
(8) -S (2, 7 Modus Tollens)
(9) -A (1, 8 Modus Tollens)

The above argument reads as follows: (1) If it is the case that agnosticism in Biblical interpretation is the correct epistemological position, then it follows that subjectivism in Biblical interpretation is a true position.

(2) If subjectivism in Biblical interpretation is a true position, then it is entirely possible for one party to affirm a specific proposition at the same time that another party denies the same proposition, and both be considered right.

(3) If it is possible for the same Bible proposition to

be both affirmed and denied with equal force, then any Bible proposition and its denial must be considered epistemologically equal (either both true or both false).

(4) If it is the case that any Bible proposition and its denial must be considered epistemologically equal, then it is not possible to know that the Bible's propositions are really and objectively true.

(5) It is possible to objectively know the truth or falsity of Bible propositions.

(6) Therefore, it is the case that it is false to state that a Bible proposition and its denial must be treated with equal epistemological status.

(7) Therefore, it is the case that it is false that one person can maintain the truthfulness of a Bible proposition at the same time another person maintains the denial of the same proposition and both be considered right.

(8) Therefore, it is false that subjectivism is true, and (9) it is false, therefore, to affirm that agnosticism in Biblical interpretation is a true epistemological position.

The second argument, like the first, is valid in form. It also contains true premises, which signifies that the conclusion is therefore true.

The crucial premise in the above argumentation is premise five, which states (affirms) that we can know the truth of the Bible's propositional statements. That premise, though not demonstrated in this section, is subject to demonstration as will be shown in the following chapter.

The importance of this argument, however, based on the proof of premise five which will follow, is that it contributes to yet another argument which shows that agnosticism as an epistemological stance in the discipline of Biblical interpretation is not warranted. **If it is possible to know that the propositional statements of the Bible are true or false, and that they cannot be held to be false at the same time as true (as subjectivism entails), then we can know that**

agnosticism is false in Biblical hermeneutics. This, then, is the gist of the preceding argument.

Most of the premises (e.g., 1, 2, 7, 8, 9) of the argument were also used in the previous argument, but a full explanation of each premise is in order.

<u>Premise One</u>: Simply stated, the first premise affirms that agnosticism implies subjectivism. That is to say, that given the tenets of agnosticism as true, one cannot but also affirm subjectivism.

<u>Premise Two</u>: This premise is simply definitional. By definition, subjectivism entails that a proposition can be both true and false within the same frame of reference.

<u>Premise Three</u>: This premise is also definitional. If two opposing propositions can be maintained at the same time as either both true or both false, then they must be epistemologically equal. It is, of course, contradictory, but given the truthfulness of agnosticism and subjectivism, this is the inevitable result.

<u>Premise Four</u>: This, too, is most obvious. If opposing propositions can be maintained at the same time (thus epistemologically equal), then it is **impossible** to know any Bible proposition as true.

<u>Premise Five</u>: This premise simply affirms that we can know that the Bible teaches X, where X is any true Bible proposition. It is the thesis of this present endeavor, and though not demonstrated here, will be the specific object of investigation in the chapter to follow. For the sake of convenience its truthfulness is assumed at this point.

<u>Premises Six Through Nine</u>: Each of these premises is the denial of the antecedents (via the logical move of Modus Tollens) in premises one through four. All of them are denied based upon the truthfulness of premise five.

The import of the above argument is simple. If it can be demonstrated that we can know that the Bible teaches X, where X is any true Bible proposition (premise five in the previous argument, the thesis of this book), then, through a series of Modus Tollens arguments, we can demonstrate that agnosticism as an epistemological position in Biblical hermeneutics is false.³ The proof of that proposition (premise five) will be fully set out in chapter ten. This second argument, like the first, merely demonstrates that the logical consequences of agnosticism and subjectivism are such that they ultimately deny both agnosticism and subjectivism.

The next two arguments differ from the previous two. These arguments will focus upon the implications, not just generally related to subjectivism, but more specifically related to agnosticism's denial of the basic thesis of this work [i.e., we cannot know that the Bible teaches X (or -KBTX)]. Each of the following two arguments, therefore, will deal with some of the implications of agnosticism's denial of that thesis.

The third argument, and the first in this second set, involves agnosticism's claim in opposition to the general thesis of this work. That thesis, which states that it is possible to know that the Bible's propositional statements are objectively true, is further involved as it relates to other implicative statements. The argument, presented in symbolic form (A = agnosticism is a true epistemological position in Biblical hermeneutics, KBTX = we can know the truth of the Bible's propositional statements, KBWG = we can know that the Bible is the word of God, KGI = we can know that God is infinite, KGE = we can know that God exists), is presented as follows:

Argument #3

(1) A > -KBTX (obvious, cf. discussion of arg.#2)
(2) -KBTX > -KBWG (see discussion)
(3) -KBWG > -KGI (see discussion)
(4) -KGI > -KGE (see discussion)
(5) KGE (see discussion and proof)
(6) KGI (4, 5 Modus Tollens)
(7) KBWG (3, 6 Modus Tollens)

(8) KBTX (2, 7 Modus Tollens)
(9) -A (1, 8 Modus Tollens)

The above argument reads as follows: (1) If agnosticism in Biblical interpretation is a true epistemological position, then it is false to affirm that we can know that the propositional statements of the Bible are objectively true, that is, it would be false to affirm that we can know the Bible teaches X, where X is any true Bible proposition.

(2) If it is false to affirm that we can know that the propositional statements of the Bible are objectively true, then it is false to affirm that we can know that the Bible is the word of God.

(3) If it is false to affirm that we can know that the Bible is the word of God, then it is false to affirm that God is infinite.

(4) If it is false to affirm that God is infinite, then it is false to affirm that God (as the Bible speaks of God) exists.

(5) But, it is true that we can know that the God of the Bible exists.

(6) Therefore it is true to affirm that we can know that God is infinite.

(7) Therefore it is true to affirm that we can know that the Bible is the word of God.

(8) Therefore it is true to affirm that we can know that the propositional statements of the Bible are true, that is to say that we can know that the Bible teaches X, where X is any true Bible proposition.

(9) It is false, therefore, to affirm that agnosticism, as it applies to an epistemological stance in Biblical interpretation, is true.

The above argument is valid in form. Furthermore, the premises which comprise the argument are true. The argument is, therefore, sound. The conclusion must then be true. But now an explanation is in order for several of the premises of the aforementioned argument.

The first premise of the argument (A > -KBTX)

simply states: If agnosticism in Biblical interpretation is a true epistemological position, then it is false to affirm that we can know that the propositional statements of the Bible are objectively true.

That implicative relationship should be self-evident, but in case it is not seen to be that way by some, notice the following argumentation which demonstrates that the first premise is a true implicative statement.

In the argument given, it must be noted that the general premises are those which were already given in argument #2. The argument in symbolic form (A = agnosticism is a true epistemological position in Biblical interpretation, S = subjectivism is a true epistemological position in Biblical interpretation, X = any Bible proposition, Z = any Bible proposition and its denial must be considered true, KBTX = we can know the truth of the Bible's propositional statements, that is to say that we can know that the Bible teaches X, where X is any true Bible proposition) is given to show that premise one of argument #3 is a true implicative statement.

(1) A > S (see previous arguments)
(2) S > (X . -X) (definitional)
(3) A > (X . -X) (1, 2 Hypothetical Syllogism)
(4) (X . -X) > Z (cf. arg. re logical contradiction)
(5) A > Z (3, 4 Hypothetical Syllogism)
(6) Z > -KBTX (obvious)
(7) A > -KBTX (5, 6 Hypothetical Syllogism)

The concluding premise of the previous argument is the same as the first premise of argument #3. It is, therefore, correct to represent the first premise of argument #3 as depicted. The preceding argument shows this to be true. Because the propositions used here have already been discussed in conjunction with previous arguments, there exists no need for further explanation of this argument.

The second premise (-KBTX > -KBWG), as with the first premise, is obvious to some, but perhaps not to others. It simply states: If we cannot know that the propositional statements of the Bible are objectively true, then we cannot know that the Bible is the word of God. That simply means that it is impossible to affirm that the Bible is God's word unless we can know that the propositional statements of the Bible are true or false. Agnosticism implies that we cannot know the propositional statements of the Bible to be objectively true or false. Thus, it is impossible, given agnosticism as a true means of epistemology in Biblical interpretation, to know that the Bible is the word of God.

This implication of agnosticism is extremely important. In the basic argument to prove that the Bible is the word of God, Thomas Warren states the following:

> As I stated earlier, our basic affirmation throughout this entire lectureship is: The Bible is the Word of God (and remember, when I say it is the word of God, I mean to say that it is inspired, inerrant, complete, powerful, authoritative). What is the basic argument in which this conclusion is drawn? Here is the argument, set out in valid argument form.
> 1. If it is the case that the Bible possesses property A, property B, property C. . . property Z (where the total situation involved in having such properties makes it clear that the Bible is beyond mere human production) then the Bible is the word of God.
> 2. It is the case that the Bible possesses property A, property B, property C. . . property Z.
> 3. Conclusion: Therefore the Bible is the word of God.
> In this argument, when I refer to

property A, property B, property C, etc., I mean for these designations to stand for affirmative propositions$_4$ regarding some fact regarding the Bible.

Note that Warren states: "In this argument...I mean for these designations to stand for affirmative propositions regarding some fact regarding the Bible." If, as per agnosticism, it is impossible to know that the propositional statements of the Bible are either true or false, then it is impossible to know that the Bible is the word of God.

According to Warren's statement, his argument to demonstrate that the Bible is the word of God is dependent upon man's ability to know certain "affirmative propositions regarding some fact regarding the Bible." Agnosticism, therefore, as it implies that we cannot know that the Bible's statements are objectively true or false, implies that we cannot know that the Bible is the word of God.

The third premise of argument #3 (-KBWG > -KGI) is also in need of some clarification. That premise states: If we cannot know that the Bible is the word of God, then we cannot know that God is infinite. Initially, this premise might be considered to be false, or, at the very least, confusing, but upon further explanation, I believe the intent of this premise will be understood.

There are two general divisions attributed to the subject of revelation, namely general and special. General revelation, or natural revelation as it is sometimes called, is that means of revelation by which the physical aspects of nature indicate the existence of God. That such is abundantly evident is seen by an examination of the world, and by a study of several Bible passages (cf. Psalm 19:1; 102:25; 139:14; Acts 14:17; 17:27; Romans 1:18-20; et. al.). Special revelation, on the other hand, has always been understood to refer to that aspect of revelation through which man received **direct** communication from God.

This has been either through a messenger of God, a vision or dream, or through the written word.

General, or natural, revelation is able to tell us many things about the existence and nature of God, but **it is not within its purview to reveal God to the fullest extent possible.** The Bible declares that "the invisible things of him from the creation of the world are clearly seen, being understood by the things that are made, even his eternal power and Godhead..." (Romans 1:20), and "Nevertheless he left not himself without witness, in that he did good, and gave us rain from heaven, and fruitful seasons, filling our hearts with food and gladness." (Acts 14:17)

The revelation of God through the means of nature, then, is only partially revealing. We can know of his existence and, to some extent, his nature, but we cannot fully understand God through this means. It is **necessary, then, if God is to be revealed to mankind in a fuller sense, that such revelation must come through some other means than through natural revelation.** This other means is usually taken to be through special (i.e., written) revelation from God.

Though it is not within the scope of this particular section to deal extensively with the necessity of special revelation, it is important to elaborate upon it briefly at this point.[5]

That God's existence can be known through the natural world as a demonstrable fact will be noted shortly. It is important to note, however, that because the existence of all things physical depends on something other than the physical (i.e., the metaphysical) for existence, God, the eternally existent being, is referred to as non-contingent, while the world and all things physical are referred to as contingent. Most of the arguments for the existence of God involve this aspect of contingency (e.g., moral, teleological, and cosmological arguments).

It is necessary, though, that God's existence be regarded not only as non-contingent, but also as infinite. To be non-contingent, an entity must of necessity be infinite. If the entity responsible for all things physical were finite, then it would be contingent also. If it were contingent, then it could not be the means responsible for the existence of all things physical. God's infinity, therefore, is an integral facet of his existence.

The infinity of God, then, becomes the key to understanding the need for special revelation. As noted previously in the section on definitions, it is assumed for the purpose of this work that God is infinite in all of his attributes, but it serves us well to point out just how that aspect of infinity applies to the need for special revelation.

Infinity, as it applies to the attributes of God, must of necessity apply to all of God's attributes. If it is applied to all of the attributes of God with the exception of one, then in that one attribute God would be finite. If God were finite, even in one attribute, it would not be proper to deem him as infinite in the totality of his being. Infinity, therefore, applies to the love, wisdom, power, mercy, grace, presence, and justice of God (as well as applying to all other attributes of God) with equal force. To understand the necessity of special revelation further, it is important to note its relation to the infinite love and benevolence of God.

If God is an infinite being that loves, then of necessity, God must be infinite in that love. Man, created in the image of God (Genesis 1:26ff), created for the pleasure of God (Revelation 4:11), is one of the objects of the love of God. That love, which exists for the purpose of bringing man to the greatest possible state that man could attain or desire, is a giving love, an unbiased love, and an unselfish love. If God desires man to live in a special way, to do special things, and to receive special blessings from him, then God must communicate these desires to man in some special way, for they are not communicated through the means of natural revelation.

That God communicates his will for mankind through

the written word is necessitated by the infinite love and desire which God had/has for mankind. To reveal his ultimate will directly, through some miraculous means, will not suffice.

First, God, in order to be just, would have to reveal the same message, in the same manner, to every person.

Second, if God uses this method of revealing his will, each person would not have to exercise his own will to search for God as God so desires (cf. Psalm 14:2; 53:2; Acts 17:26-27).

Third, as is evidenced by the claim that so many make today with regard to receiving miraculous revelation, many differing messages would be received. If such means of revelation existed today man would need the "discerning of spirits" gift available to him in order to prove what messages were from God. But, because this does not exist today, there is no way to objectively verify the truth of these numerous and differing messages.

On the other hand, if God revealed himself through the written word, such communication is subject to objective and reliable verification, and without a miraculous element involved. Though it is not within the objectives of this section to demonstrate this aspect of revelation, it will be discussed in the following chapter which deals with the positive argumentation of the thesis. Suffice it so say at this point, that God chose to reveal himself through the best method possible, which revelation was necessitated because of the infinite love of God.

To state, therefore, as the third premise states, that we cannot know that God is infinite if the Bible is not the word of God, is to say that some form of special revelation from God to man was necessary for God to reveal his full love and complete will to man. Furthermore, it also indicates that such revelation from God to man was necessary for the salvation of man. If it was necessary for the salvation of man, and if God did not provide that revelation, then God would not be infinite in love, wisdom, power, or some other aspect of his attributes.

The fourth premise of argument #3 (-KGI > -KGE) is also in need of some explanation, but not to the extent as the previous premises.

That premise states: If we cannot know that God is infinite, then God (as the Bible speaks of God) does not exist. As indicated previously in the chapter devoted to definitions, God, as the Bible speaks of God and as this work addresses God, is infinite in all of his nature. To capitulate, therefore, to a finite "God" is to deny the existence of the God of the Bible. To admit finitude with respect to the nature of God might be perfectly acceptable to the process theologian, but it does not prove acceptable to the Biblical theist. It is therefore self-evident to state that the finitude of God is tantamount to denying the existence of God.

The fifth premise of argument #3 (KGE), which states that we can know that God exists, is the most crucial premise of the argument. If it can be demonstrated that God does in fact exist, then that propositional truth supplies evidence to negate the antecedents of the previous premises, that is, it serves to affirm that we can know that God is infinite, that the Bible is the word of God, and that we can know that the Bible teaches propositional truth which is subject to human cognition. Furthermore, proof of the existence of God will serve to demonstrate that agnosticism, as an epistemological stance in the discipline of Biblical hermeneutics, is a completely untenable position.

It is absolutely necessary therefore, though this work is not devoted to the sole purpose of demonstrating the existence of God, to mention at least one form of argumentation which yields the proposition that God exists as its conclusion.

As mentioned in the preceding paragraphs, many of the arguments usually offered in defense of the existence of God are based on the element of contingency. Space prohibits a full explanation of the

arguments based upon contingency, but they usually follow the succeeding form.
(1) If anything contingent exists, then something non-contingent must exist.
(2) Contingent things do exist.
(3) Therefore, something non-contingent must exist.

This argument may seem over-simplified, but the force of it is not to be overlooked. The argument is valid, being Modus Ponens in form, and the premises are true. The argument must then be sound, which therefore necessitates the truthfulness of the conclusion.

Though the above argument states the form of contingency in a very general way, the following argumentation expands that argument in a way that deals specifically with the elements of contingency.

Proposition 1: The world of nature is an actually existing world which includes within itself the real things and events we find by means of our experience. . . .

Proposition 2: Any such world of actually existing things and events is a world which is neither self-existent nor contains anything self-existent as a part of itself. . . .

Proposition 3: The world of nature is a world which neither exists by itself nor contains anything self-existent as a part of itself. . . .

Proposition 4: Whatever neither exists by itself nor contains anything self-existent as a part of itself depends for its existence upon something which does exist in and of itself and does not in turn depend on anything else. . . .

Proposition 5: Anything which depends for its existence on something which is self-existent depends for its existence upon a really existing God. . . .

Proposition 6: <u>Anything which is not self-existent depends for its existence upon a really existing God.</u>
Proposition 7: <u>The world of nature depends for its existence upon a really existing God.</u>[6]

The above argument, as set forth by Samuel M. Thompson, contains seven categorical propositions, which when broken down into three separate categorical syllogisms, render the conclusion that the existence of this physical world is dependent for its existence upon a really existing God. That argumentation is set forth in the subsequent formulation:

(1) A(d) < B(u)
(2) B(d) < C(u)
(3) A(d) < C(u)
(4) C(d) < D(u)
(5) D(d) < E(u)
(6) C(d) < E(u)
(7) A(d) < E(u)

This set of propositions breaks down into the following three valid categorical syllogisms, as previously noted.

Argument A

(1) A(d) < B(u)
(2) B(d) < C(u)
(3) A(d) < C(u)

Argument B

(4) C(d) < D(u)
(5) D(d) < E(u)
(6) C(d) < E(u)

The third argument is comprised of propositions three and six which yield premise seven as the conclusion.

Argument C

(3) $A(d) < C(u)$
(6) $\underline{C(d) < E(u)}$
(7) $\overline{A(d) < E(u)}$

Each of the above arguments is valid. Each consists of A-type propositions, each of which is true, which results in three sound arguments. The conclusions, then, of each of the arguments are true. The significance of the preceding argument is overwhelming. Its conclusion states that the physical world as we know it depends for its existence upon a self-existing God. The argument, therefore, provides the demonstrable proof needed to sustain the existence of God.

Having proven the existence of God, it is evident that premise five of argument #3 is true. Having demonstrated the truthfulness of premise 5, it follows, through a series of Modus Tollens arguments (see argument #3, premises 6-9), that we can know that God is infinite in his nature, that we can know that the Bible is the word of God, and that we can know that the Bible teaches propositional statements which we can know to be objectively true. From these arguments we are able to demonstrate that agnosticism, which through its implicative nature demanded the denial of these truths, is false.

Argument #3, therefore, conclusively demonstrates that agnosticism as an epistemological position in Biblical interpretation is totally without foundation. That conclusion rests soundly upon the existence of the one true God of the Bible, which existence necessitates the negation of the logical implications of hermeneutical agnosticism.

---

1. Note this explanation as it applies to the previous section, pages 78-81.

2. cf. p. 58, fn. 18

3. The same conclusion can also be obtained through a simple disjunctive syllogism. [e.g. A v -A; -(-A); A]

4. Thomas B. Warren, "The Bible Is God's Word-The Meaning And Basic Argument For This Claim," <u>The Inspiration And Authority Of The Bible-1971 Bible Lectureship Of Harding Graduate School Of Religion</u> eds. W.B. West, Jr., B. Flatt, T.B. Warren (Nashville: Gospel Advocate, 1971), pp. 17-18

5. For a more detailed explanation of the necessity of special, propositional revelation see chapter ten.

6. Samuel M. Thompson, <u>A Modern Philosophy Of Religion</u> (Chicago: Henry Regnery Company, 1955), pp. 285-286

7. For a thorough explanation of the significance, rules, etc. of categorical syllogisms, see chapters seven and eight of Lionel Ruby, <u>Logic: An Introduction</u>, pp. 154-204.

CHAPTER NINE-C:

ARGUMENTATION AGAINST AGNOSTICISM

Argument # 4, the last argument to be presented in this section, deals with one more **specific implication** of the agnostic position. This argument deals with the implications considered in chapter eight ("Examples Of The Problem") regarding marriage, divorce, and remarriage. It furthermore deals with the general subject of **salvation** in light of the **implications of the doctrine of hermeneutical agnosticism.**
That argument in symbolic form (A = agnosticism as an epistemological position in Biblical interpretation is a true position, KBTX = we can know that the Bible teaches propositional statements which can be known to be objectively true or false, KMDR = we can know the truth of the Bible's teaching concerning marriage, divorce, and remarriage, SSIKWTDFS = there are souls in sin and it is impossible for them (or anyone else) to know what they need to do or know in order to be saved, GHGUANFS = God has given us all that is necessary for our soul's salvation, KGIL = we can know that God is infinite in love, KGI = we can know that God is infinite, and KGE = we can know that God exists) is set forth as follows:

Argument #4

(1) A > -KBTX (cf. arg. #3)
(2) -KBTX > -KMDR (see discussion)
(3) -KMDR > SSIKWTDFS (see discussion)
(4) SSIKWTDFS > -GHGUANFS (see discussion)
(5) -GHGUANFS > -KGIL (see discussion)
(6) -KGIL > -KGI (obvious)
(7) -KGI > -KGE (obvious)
(8) KGE (cf. Thompson's arg.)
(9) KGI (7, 8 Modus Tollens)

(10) KGIL (6, 9 Modus Tollens)
(11) GHGUANFS (5, 10 Modus Tollens)
(12) -SSIKWTDFS (4, 11 Modus Tollens)
(13) KMDR (3, 12 Modus Tollens)
(14) KBTX (2, 13 Modus Tollens)
(15) -A (1, 14 Modus Tollens)

The above argument reads as follows: (1) If agnosticism in Biblical interpretation is a true epistemological position, then it is false to affirm that we can know that the propositional statements of the Bible are objectively true or false.

(2) If it is false to affirm that we can know that the propositional statements of the Bible are objectively true or false, then it is false to claim that we can know the truth of the Bible's teachings regarding marriage, divorce, and remarriage.

(3) If it is false to claim that we can know the truth of the Bible's teachings concerning marriage, divorce, and remarriage, then it is the case that there are souls in sin and it is impossible for them (or anyone else) to know what they need to do in order to be saved.

(4) If it is the case that there are souls in sin and it is impossible for them (or anyone else) to know what they need to do to be saved, then it is false to affirm that God has given us all that is necessary for our soul's salvation.

(5) If it is false to affirm that God has given us all that is necessary for our soul's salvation, then it is false to affirm that God is infinite in love.

(6) If it is false to affirm that God is infinite in love, then it is false to affirm that God is infinite (i.e., completely infinite).

(7) If it is false to affirm that God is infinite, then it is false to affirm that God (as the Bible speaks of God) exists.

(8) But, it is true that we can know that the God of the Bible exists.

(9) It is, therefore, possible to know that God is

infinite.

(10) It is, therefore, possible to know that God is infinite in love.

(11) It is, therefore, possible to know and affirm that God has given us all that we need for our soul's salvation.

(12) It is, therefore, false to affirm that there are souls in sin and it is impossible for them (or anyone else) to know what they need to do in order to be saved.

(13) We can, therefore, know the truth of the Bible's teachings on marriage, divorce, and remarriage.

(14) Therefore, we can know that the propositional statements of the Bible are objectively true or false, that is to say that we can know that the Bible teaches X, where X is any true Bible proposition.

(15) It is false, then, to affirm that agnosticism as an epistemological position in Biblical interpretation is correct.

The above argument is valid in form. Furthermore, the premises which comprise the argument are true. The argument, then, is sound. The conclusion must necessarily follow.

An explanation of the argument is in order to avoid any difficulty in understanding the premises and the conclusion.

The first premise (A > -KBTX) is the same premise noted in argument #3. For a discussion of this premise, please note the remarks made previously (cf. pp. 89 ff.).

The second premise (-KBTX > -KMDR) should be obvious. It reads: If it is false to affirm that we can know that the propositional statements of the Bible are objectively true (or false), then it is false to claim that we can know the truth of the Bible's teachings regarding marriage, divorce, and remarriage. The consequent of this premise simply follows from the antecedent. If the premise is true, then it is the case that the consequent follows. Given agnosticism as an epistemological position in Biblical hermeneutics, the antecedent is true, and the consequent follows. As a matter of fact, if we cannot know that the Bible teaches X, where X is any true Bible proposition (i.e., to deny that we can objectively know the propositional statements of the Bible as either true or false), then **it is impossible to know ANYTHING about the Bible.**

The third premise (-KMDR > SSIKWTDFS) states: If it is false to affirm that we can know the truth of the Bible's teachings concerning marriage, divorce, and remarriage, then it is the case that there are souls in sin and it is impossible for them (or anyone else) to know what they need to do for their soul's salvation.

This premise, given agnosticism as a true epistemological position in hermeneutics, must be true. If we cannot know the truth about the Bible's teaching on any subject that is absolutely vital to the salvation of souls (such as marriage, divorce, and remarriage), then it is an inescapable conclusion that there exist many souls which must of necessity know the truth about this subject (or any other vital subject), but which, due to an agnostic approach in Biblical interpretation, **do not,** indeed **cannot,** know the truth about this matter. Joe Barnett's article "Throwaway Marriages," alluded to in chapter eight, correctly acknowledges the problem of marriage, divorce, and remarriage in the United States. Indeed, many are the statistical studies that have concluded that such problems have increased drastically in the last several decades. If these studies are accurate, and no one doubts that they are, then individuals involved in such relationships are **also involved in situations about which they cannot know the proper answers in order to obtain salvation.** Barnett, by listing only "possible solutions" to the problem of interpreting Matthew 19:9, has given no hope to these individuals. Such are the consequences of hermeneutical agnosticism.

The fourth premise (SSIKWTDFS > -GHGUANFS) simply states: If there are souls in sin and it is impossible for them (or anyone else) to know what they need to do in order to be saved, then it is false to

- 105 -

affirm that God has given us all that is necessary for our soul's salvation. God, as earlier mentioned, wants all men to be saved (II Peter 3:9; I Timothy 2:4). If, however, it is impossible for souls in sin to know what they must do in order to obtain salvation, then God must be to blame. Man, after all, cannot be held responsible for something which he cannot know.

The fifth premise (-GHGUANFS > -KGIL) states: If it is false to affirm that God has given us all that is necessary for our soul's salvation, then it is false to affirm that God is infinite in love. In connection with the necessity of divine revelation, we have already discussed the infinity of God (cf. pp. 93 ff.). God, due to his necessary existence, must of necessity be infinite in all respects. To be finite, even in one aspect, is to deny the totally infinite God of the Bible. To be infinite, then, entails that God is infinite in love as well as all of his other attributes. But, if the antecedent of premise five is true, that is, if God has not given us all that is necessary for our salvation, then God could not possibly be infinite in love.

The sixth premise (-KGIL > -KGI) simply states: If it is false to say that God is infinite in love, then it is false to say that God is infinite. As explained previously, this statement is obvious. God, if finite in just one aspect of his nature, would be less than infinite, and thus only finite in his total being. The aspect of infinity entails that God is infinite in all of his characteristics which comprise his nature.

The seventh premise (-KGI > -KGE) is the same as premise four in argument #3 (cf. pp. 97 ff.). It states: If it is false to affirm that God is infinite, then it is false to affirm that God (as the Bible speaks of God) exists. As mentioned in the chapter devoted to definitions, God, as the Bible speaks of God, and as this work speaks of God, is infinite in all of his nature. To capitulate to the concept of a finite "God" is to deny the God of the Bible. It is, therefore, definitional and self-evident to state that the finitude of "God" is tantamount to denying the existence of

God.

The eighth premise (KGE) simply states that we can know that the God of the Bible exists. Proof of this premise has already been given (cf. pp. 97 ff.). This premise, and its proof, provide the necessary means to deny the antecedents of premises one through seven. Premise eight, as it proves the consequent of premise seven to be false, that is at it proves that God exists, furthermore proves:

(1) that God is infinite,
(2) that God is infinite in love,
(3) that God has given us all that is necessary for our soul's salvation,
(4) that it is false to affirm that there are souls in sin and that it is impossible for them to know what to do for their soul's salvation,
(5) that it is true to affirm that we can know the truth of the Bible's teachings regarding marriage, divorce, and remarriage,
(6) that it is true to affirm that we can know that the propositional statements of the Bible are objectively true, and finally,
(7) that we can know that agnosticism as a means of epistemology in Biblical interpretation is a false hermeneutical approach. All of these affirmations come from a series of Modus Tollens arguments (cf. premises 9-15 of argument #4).

Each of the preceding four arguments (chapters 9-B and 9-C) yielded the conclusion that agnosticism, as an epistemological position in the realm of Biblical hermeneutics, is an untenable and indefensible position. Furthermore, though this aspect was only briefly included in the argumentation, it must be pointed out that the implications of agnosticism in hermeneutics are far reaching.

Some of the **implications** of agnosticism mentioned in these arguments are:

(1) We cannot know that the Bible is the word of God.
(2) We cannot know that God is infinite.

(3) We cannot know that God exists.

(4) We cannot know that the propositional statements of the Bible are objectively true or false, that is to say that we cannot know X, where X is any true Bible proposition.

(5) We cannot know the truth of the Bible's teachings concerning marriage, divorce, and remarriage.

(6) We cannot know what to tell those souls involved in marriage, divorce, and remarriage situations to do.

(6) We cannot know that God has given us all that is necessary for our soul's salvation.

(7) We cannot know that God is infinite in love.

It can be readily seen that the implications of hermeneutical agnosticism are ominous. Biblical theism, which denies that these implications are true, is called upon to give defense of its thesis, and to deny that hermeneutical agnosticism is true. The following chapter will present positive argumentation in defense of the thesis which states: **We can know whether or not the propositional statements of the Bible are objectively true or false, that is to say that we can know that the Bible teaches X, where X is any true Bible proposition.**

CHAPTER TEN:

ARGUMENTATION IN DEFENSE OF THE THESIS

Having thoroughly discussed, and refuted, the negative implications of hermeneutical agnosticism, it becomes necessary to set forth the positive case in defense of the thesis of this work. That thesis, as has been mentioned, simply states: **It is possible for man to know or understand all that the Bible teaches regarding that which is necessary for the salvation of one's soul.**

In a very real sense, the positive argumentation began in the previous chapters. By denying the consequences of agnosticism in hermeneutics, we demonstrated that the epistemological status of agnosticism was not at all warranted or tenable. By doing such, we tacitly demonstrated that the thesis of this work was true. Note the following simple disjunction which illustrates this (A = agnosticism in Biblical interpretation is the correct means of epistemological approach to Bible study, O/T(jla) = objectivism (or the thesis proposed by this author) is the correct means of epistemological approach to understanding the truths taught within the Bible):

(1) A v O/T(jla) (an obvious disjunction)
(2) -A (as demonstrated in chapter nine)
(3) O/T(jla) (1, 2 Disjunctive Syllogism)

The above argument would read as follows: (1) Either agnosticism in hermeneutics is the true epistemological position, **or** objectivism (the thesis of this author) is the true epistemological position in Biblical interpretation.

(2) Agnosticism **is not** the true epistemological position in hermeneutics (as evidenced by the arguments presented in the preceding chapter of this work).

(3) Therefore, it is the case that objectivism (the thesis of this book) is the correct and true

epistemological position in Biblical interpretation.

With reference to the above approach to understanding the Bible, note the following series of disjuncts as set forth by Thomas B. Warren:

> At this point I should like to set out four disjunctive (alternative) propositions: (1) either subjectivism is the correct approach in seeking the truth or objectivism is the correct approach; (2) either there is some objective standard (to which all men have obligation) or there is no such objective standard; (3) either men can know (both <u>that</u> it is and <u>what</u> it is) the objective standard or men cannot know the objective standard; and (4) either the Bible is that objective standard or it is not.[1]

The above statement indicates a basic approach which must be considered. Generally speaking, **either** a subjective approach (represented by agnosticism) **or** an objective approach (represented by this thesis) must be maintained in Biblical interpretation. The previous section has amply demonstrated the weaknesses of the subjective approach (agnosticism), and we have already indicated that the denial of either of the conjuncts in the disjunctive syllogism warrants the conclusion that the remaining conjunct is true.[2] Thus, the first positive argument in defense of this thesis has, in a sense, already been presented and examined.

The remainder of this chapter, therefore, will deal with specific arguments which demonstrate the truthfulness of the thesis.

Positive Argumentation Of The Thesis

One of the most basic foundations upon which Christianity rests is that teaching which affirms that

God can communicate. This tenet of Christian doctrine is so fundamental and intrinsically related to Christianity that many have merely assumed its truthfulness without further thought. Though it is, indeed, correct to believe it is true, without having good reason to do so can be dangerous. With this in mind, it shall be the thrust of this section to examine the communicative ability of God.

First, most critics who question the communicative ability of God do not question their own communicative ability, or the communicative ability of their fellow man. It would be safe to say that these critics all take for granted that communication can, and does, occur between human beings. To contend otherwise would be temerarious. Why, then, is it so unusual to affirm that God, who created men that can communicate, can communicate too?

The Bible addresses this matter of God's communicative ability. Moses, when he complained to the Lord of his own inadequacy in speech, was rebuked by the Lord, who said: "Who hath made man's mouth? or who maketh the dumb, or deaf, or the seeing, or the blind? have not I the Lord?" (Exodus 4:11) The writer of Proverbs answered the question with: "The hearing ear, and the seeing eye, the Lord hath made even both of them." (Proverbs 20:12) What is the conclusion, then, to this line of thought? Quite simply: "He that planted the ear, shall he not hear? He that formed the eye, shall he not see?" (Psalm 94:9) We might continue by asking: "He that formed the tongue, shall he not speak?" It seems, then, quite plain that the Bible teaches that God can communicate.

Second, many critics simply do not understand that the Bible not only teaches that God can communicate, but that this ability is one distinguishable feature which sets the one true God apart from the "gods" of the heathen world. The great contest between Elijah and the prophets of Baal rendered this conclusion most beautifully (I Kings 17:20-40). In this instance, God responded to the call of Elijah, and communicated his will by consuming the burnt sacrifices, the wood, the stones, the dust, and the water within the trench. The heathen "gods" could not do this, for they could neither hear nor be heard.

This, too, is the earnest contention of Isaiah. God, unlike the dumb idols of stone and wood who had to be carried from place to place, was a God that "hath **declared** from the beginning" (Isaiah 41:26); that was able to **declare** "new things...before they spring forth" (42:9); and that said "Fear ye not, neither be afraid: have not I **told** thee from that time, and have **declared** it? ye are even my witnesses. Is there a God beside me? yea, there is no God; I know not any." (44:8) What was Isaiah's point? No "god" could communicate like the one true God! In fact, no "god" could communicate at all, not to mention his inability to communicate what would happen in the future.

God, therefore, can communicate. This is the basic contention of the Bible. His ability to create men that can communicate, as well as his infinite nature, both demand the conclusion that God can communicate. The big question, however, upon coming to the conclusion that God can communicate is **"how does God communicate?"**

Many religionists have contended that God communicates **immediately** to the believer. To communicate immediately is to communicate directly, that is without a medium of communication (e.g., without written or oral communication). This is the position advocated by John Baillie in his book <u>Our Knowledge Of God</u>.[3] In this book, Baillie contends that man cannot know God by inferential argument, but rather only through God's **immediate** revelation to us. Thus, Baillie rejects natural theology (i.e., natural revelation), as well as rejecting the Scriptures as propositional truth.

Others have maintained that God communicates mediately, that is through the physical world. John Hick, for instance, argues that "Many of the Biblical writers were (sometimes, though doubtless not at all times) as vividly conscious of being in God's presence as they were of living in a material environment."[4] His point is that the believer does not claim that God comes to him in all his majesty (i.e., immediately as Baillie suggested), but rather that God comes to him in and through the material and social realms.[5]

Still others maintain that though God has communicated in the past through immediate means (e.g., dreams, visions, or through actual speech, etc.), he now only reveals his will through propositional, that is written, revelation. Though it is beyond the scope of this present work to examine in detail each of these alternatives, it is important to discuss them briefly.

If it is true that God communicates only immediately, that is directly to the mind of every believer, several problems are evident.

First, why does he not communicate to all men? If God is not a respecter of persons (Acts 10:34; Romans 2:11), would he not, therefore, communicate to all men?

Second, why is it that among those who contend for such immediate revelation there exists no unanimity of doctrine? Why does one contend that God communicated unto him "X," while another maintains that God communicated unto him "Y?" If God communicates his will immediately, why is it not the case that he communicates the same will to every person? These questions, though just scratching the surface of the issue, are most crucial. If these inconsistencies abound in this alleged form of communication, it seems most appropriate to abandon it.

Next, if it is true that God communicates mediately, that is through the existing physical world, why is it not the case that **this** form of revelation occurs to every person? If, because of the existing world, it is self-evident that God exists, why are there those who claim that God does not exist?

Furthermore, if God communicates through the physical world, **how does he do so** and **how can we**

know what that communication is? The pantheist looks at the world and sees one thing, but the atheist examines the world and sees something completely different. Even if it were granted, for the sake of argument, that **everyone** knew of God's existence from the naturally existing world, **what does that same world tell us about how God wants us to live?** Historically, some have assumed that the physical nature of man's existence was so completely separate from his spiritual nature, that it was man's duty to abstain from physical pleasures as much as possible. This lead to asceticism. Others, beginning with the same emphasis upon the separation of that which is physical from that which is spiritual, were lead to believe that one could do whatever he desired in his physical body and not affect his true spiritual nature. This lead to libertinism. Thus, the same view of the relationship between the physical and the spiritual natures of man produced asceticism by those who sought to abstain from the flesh, or libertinism by those who sought to revel in the flesh. If God reveals himself mediately, why is there no unanimity of teaching among men? As you can see, some of the same criticisms lodged against immediate revelation can also be lodged against mediate revelation.

The remaining possibility, that of propositional revelation, is the position maintained by this writer, and is, indeed, the position advocated by the Bible. It is not, however, without its critics, as further discussion (cf. chapter eleven) will show. It is, though, the only means of revelation that does not present God as a respecter of persons, that recognizes the free will of man, and that maintains objectivity in human understanding.

It is no accident, then, that God chose to communicate his will through language. Dr. J.D. Thomas notes the following concerning this important subject:

> Linguistic communication is the most

common method of sharing ideas used by human beings, perhaps because it is the most precise and the least ambiguous. By this we mean that words, expressed in sentences with subjects and predicates, and carrying propositional statements of cognitive, rational ideas, are the best means of one's mind communicating with another, and this is no doubt why language was invented. Men think in terms that have propositional content, and they impart cognitive information to each other. These propositions are intellectually grasped and are reflected by reason, up to the point that they are understood and a judgment is formed, which also can then be stated propositionally.[6]

This points out the method of communicating our thoughts and ideas on a day-to-day basis, but the same principle is also true with regard to God's communicative ability through the Bible. Thomas continues by saying:

We sometimes speak of "non-verbal communication," and it does exist, but it is more susceptible to ambiguity than is word-revelation. Again, one school of theology argues that God revealed His will in events, not words, and that we therefore need to concern ourselves with proper understanding of God's acts in history. (This view is because they feel that the word-revelation of the Bible cannot be God's true revelation.) The trouble with revelation by events only, is the likelihood of misinterpretation. For instance, the event of Christ's crucifixion was interpreted differently by the Roman soldiers who put Jesus to death from what it was by the disciples of the Lord. It needs word-revelation to make it precise and definite for all alike. Unless God has used words in propositional statements in making His will known, man is in a complete sea of confusion. There is no way that man could know sufficient details if revelation is only by events.

Both normal communication and the Bible are therefore in cognitive, propositional form, and they impart information that is understandable by reason. The same message is understandable alike by more than one mind, and therefore the word-revelation is objective public truth. Every normal man stands equal before the revelation, and the message that it conveys is applicable to all alike. The Bible presents a plan of salvation, for instance, that can be responded to by every responsible person, and every man can have the salvation provided by Christ, on equal terms.[7]

Clark Pinnock echoes Thomas in affirming the following about propositional word-revelation:

God's <u>Word</u> is central in the biblical concept of divine revelation. Pagan idols are dumb, but the Lord is a living, speaking God. Revelation is mediated through language. Man and God have become speech partners. Language is the basis of culture, and written language is durable, objective and transmissible. Scripture grew out of the divine speaking as it was cast into writing for the welfare of God's people. God-inspired Scripture is an extension of the modality of the divine speaking. Writing has revelational significance in the Bible. Moses wrote down the law for a witness (Deut. 31:24-26). Scripture was written for our learning (Ro. 15:4). John was ordered to write (Rev. 1:1). The New Testament phrase "it is written" is the equivalent of saying "Thus saith the Lord."

"What Scripture says, God says." The divine Word is cast into permanent form in Scripture, which is the durable vehicle of special revelation and provides the conceptual framework in which we meet and comprehend God. . . . . . Our encounter with God takes place within the context of mutual knowledge.

The word-deed complex in divine revelation must not be shattered. God did not act without speaking, nor speak without acting. His mighty deeds of redemption are clothed with a word of interpretation. "Christ died (act) for our sins (meaning)" (I Co. 15:3).[8]

What, then, is the importance of word-revelation. Alexander Campbell sums it up by saying:

> But the fact, that God has clothed his communications in human language, and that he has spoken by men, to men is <u>prima facie</u> evidence that he is to be understood, as one man conversing with another. Righteousness, or what we sometimes call <u>honesty</u> requires this; for unless he first made a special stipulation when he began to speak, his words were, in all candor, to be taken at the current value;...
> As then, there is no divine dictionary, grammar, or special rules of interpretation

for the Bible, then that book, to be understood, must be submitted to the common dictionary, grammar, and rules of language in which it was written; and as a living language is constantly fluctuating, the true and proper meaning of the words and sentences of the Bible, must be learned from the acceptation of those words and phrases, in the times and countries in which it was written. In all this, there is nothing special; for Diodorus, Herodotus, Josephus, Philo, Tacitus, Sallust, etc., and all the writers of all languages, ages, and nations, are translated and understood in the same manner.

Enthusiasts and fanatics of all ages, determine the meaning of words, from that knowledge of things which they imagine themselves to possess, rather than from the words of the author,—"They decide by what they suppose he ought to mean, rather than by what he says."

To adopt any other course, or to apply any other rules, would necessarily divest the sacred writings of every attribute that belongs to the idea of revelation. It must never be forgotten in perusing the Bible, that in the structure of sentences, in the figures of speech, in the arrangement and use of words, it differs not at all from other writings, and must, therefore, be understood and interpreted as they are.[9]

Campbell's point is clear. The Bible, like other forms of communication, must be taken as if it were intended to be a means of understandable communication. We have nothing within the Bible, or any other source, which would demand that the Bible was not written to be understood. We might ask, however, what the consequences would be if the Bible were not subject to objective understanding. Thomas Warren notes:

> Can we learn (come to knowledge of) what the Bible teaches? If we cannot, then even if the Bible is absolute truth (which it is), then the Bible is not even a revelation to man! If no man can understand the Bible (and know that he understands it), then of what value would the Bible be (to man)? None whatsoever. In contrast to the agnostics among us (who claim that it is arrogant to claim to know truth), Jesus said, "Ye shall know the truth, and the truth shall make you free." (John 8:32.) The agnostics among us, in self-contradiction, claim to know that no one knows that any propositions of religion are true.[10]

Of the three possibilities initially suggested, only the concept of propositional word-revelation statements is conceivable. Both immediate and mediate revelational theories have such difficulties attributable to them that they could not possibly be the form of communication that is represented in the Bible. When we speak, therefore, of God's communication, we will understand it to refer to propositional word-revelation statements.

The question yet remains: Can God's word, even if it is in the form of propositional statements, be understood by man? As we begin the formal argumentation in defense of the thesis, the answer will become increasingly clear. **Yes, God's word, made in propositional statements, can be understood by man.**

Argument #1

(1) (KP . XSHK . IMPTCX) > KX
(2) KP (see discussion to follow)

(3) XSHK (see discussion to follow)
(4) IMPTCX (see discussion to follow)
(5) (KP . XSHK . IMPTCX) (2, 3, 4 Conj.)
(6) KX (1, 5 Modus Ponens)

Argument #2

(1) (KP . BXSHK . IMPTCBX) > KBTX
(2) KP (see discussion to follow)
(3) BXSHK (see discussion to follow)
(4) IMPTCBX (see discussion to follow)
(5) (KP . BXSHK . IMPTCBX) (2, 3, 4 Conj.)
(6) KBTX (1, 5 Modus Ponens)

The arguments given above in symbolic form are both similar. The key to understanding them is as follows: KP = knowledge is possible, XSHK = X, which represents any proposition, is subject to human knowledge, IMPTCX = an individual has the mental potential to conceive X; KX = one can know X. In the second argument, the meanings are almost identical: KP = knowledge is possible, BXSHK = a true Bible proposition X, which is subject to human knowledge, IMPTCBX = an individual has the mental potential to conceive what the Bible teaches about X, and KBTX = we can know what the Bible teaches about X.

The first argument is simply a general argument which yields as its conclusion the proposition that we can know that which is indeed subject to knowledge. In word form it is as follows:

(1) If human knowledge is possible, and if any given subject (e.g., X) is subject to human knowledge, and if a specific individual has the mental potential to conceive that subject (X), then that subject (X) can be known.
(2) Human knowledge is possible.
(3) The specific subject (X) under consideration is subject to human knowledge.
(4) The individual under consideration does have the

mental potential to conceive this subject (X).

(5) Therefore, human knowledge is possible, and this subject (X) is subject to human knowledge, and this individual does have the mental potential to conceive/understand the subject (X).

(6) This subject (X), then, is knowable.[11]

The wording of the argument might seem awkward, but it does take into account all of the necessary variables. First, before anything else should be considered, we must question whether or not knowledge is possible. As indicated in the introductory chapters of this work, the attainment of knowledge is assumed possible. It must be the case, however, that such a conclusion is demonstrable. Note the following argument.

Argument #1-A

(1) K v -K (Law of Excluded Middle)
(2) -K > -(K v -K)
(3) K (2, 1 Modus Tollens)

This argument has but one variable: K = knowledge is possible. The argument reads: (1) Either knowledge is possible **or** knowledge is not possible.

(2) If knowledge is not possible, then it is not possible to know whether or not premise one (K v -K) is true or false.

(3) But, because such would be a denial of the law of excluded middle, which is an undeniable axiomatic truth, we must conclude, therefore, that knowledge is possible.

The preceding argument is most telling. Any disjunction which contains two completely opposite conjuncts such as K and -K, must of necessity be true. To maintain a proposition, then, which denies that which must of necessity be true, is to maintain a false proposition. If "knowledge is possible" and "knowledge is not possible" are completely opposite conjuncts (which they are), then to maintain that knowledge is not possible is to maintain that we cannot know that "knowledge is possible or knowledge is not possible" is a true statement. Knowledge, therefore, must be possible. This is the proof, then, of premise two in arguments #1 and #2.[12]

The third premise in each of the two arguments given has to do with the cognition of any given subject. In order to be understood by man, a specific subject must be able to be known by man. If it is beyond the realm of human cognition, then, certainly, we cannot rightly claim to know it. This premise is self-evident in both arguments.

The fourth premise in each of the two arguments given deals with the mental potential of the individual under consideration. It, too, is an obvious proposition. In order for a thing to be known, first it must be subject to human knowledge (premise three), but second, it must also be conceived by an individual subject that has the mental potential to conceive that topic. Needless to say, an imbecile cannot fathom Einstein's theory of relativity. This is not to say, however, that such cannot be understood, but rather that the understanding is only available to those with the potential to understand that given subject.

If the second, third, and fourth premises in each of the preceding arguments are true, then it necessarily follows that premise five, which is the conjunction of these three premises, is also true in each argument. If premise five is true, then the antecedent of premise one is true, and the consequent necessarily follows by Modus Ponens. The conclusion in each of the above arguments is therefore true.

In the first argument, the conclusion is simply that a knowledge of some specific subject is possible. In the second argument, the conclusion is that some specific subject taught in the Bible is subject to human knowledge. Both of these arguments are general in that they are premised upon general propositions: (1) knowledge is possible, (2) the subject under consideration must be subject to knowledge, and (3) the individual under consideration must have the mental potential to conceive the subject. If the arguments were to yield the conclusion that a specific subject matter (in the world or in the Bible) were knowable, then the premises would have to reflect that same degree of specificity. The conclusion can never outrun the evidence.

It is essential, then, to provide further argumentation which yields specific conclusions.

Argument #3

(1) KBWG > KBTX (see discussion to follow)
(2) KBWG (see discussion to follow)
(3) KBTX (1, 2 Modus Ponens)

The above argument, set out in symbolic terms, has as its conclusion the proposition that we can know that the Bible teaches X, where X is any true Bible proposition, which conclusion is the thesis of this work. In order to understand the argument further, it is important that the argument be explained. (KEY: KBWG = man can know that the Bible is the word of God, KBTX = man can know that the Bible teaches X, where X is any true Bible proposition)

The argument reads as follows: (1) If we can know that the Bible is the word of God, then we can know that the Bible teaches X, where X is any true Bible proposition.

(2) We can know that the Bible is the word of God.

(3) Therefore, we can know that the Bible teaches X, where X is any true Bible proposition.

As the argument presently stands, it is valid in form. The soundness of the argument depends, of course, upon the truthfulness of its premises. We must, therefore, examine both premises of the argument; premise one to see whether or not a true implicative relationship exists between the antecedent and the consequent, and premise two to determine whether or not we can know that the Bible really is the word of God.

Premise one (KBWG > KBTX) simply states: If we can know that the Bible is the word of God, then we can know that the Bible teaches X, where X is any true Bible proposition. This premise is most crucial to understand.

The reader may notice that this proposition is logically equivalent, via transposition, to premise two in argument #3 (cf. chapter 9-B, pp. 89ff). That proposition (-KBTX > -KBWG) states: If it is false to affirm that the propositional statements of the Bible are objectively true or false, then it is false to affirm that we can know that the Bible is the word of God. This simply means that it is impossible to affirm that the Bible is God's word if we can not know that the propositional statements of the Bible are true or false.

The importance of this implicative relationship was noted in the context of discussing argument #3 (chapter 9-B), but worthy of mention once again. In order to know that the Bible is the word of God, **it must be possible to know and understand certain facts about the Bible which, when assimilated into a deductive argument, produce evidence that the Bible is of divine origin.** Without the ability to know these facts, one CAN NOT KNOW that the Bible is the word of God. Thus, if one can not know that the Bible is the word of God BECAUSE he <u>can not know</u> that the Bible's propositional statements are either true or false (i.e., -KBTX > -KBWG), it follows (by transposition) that IF one <u>can know</u> that the Bible is the word of God, that he <u>can know</u> that the Bible's propositional statements are either true or false (i.e., KBWG > KBTX).

The nature of the Bible is such that certain facts about the Bible demand its divine origin. To say, then, that the Bible is the word of God is to affirm that these facts (propositional statements) are true. If one fully understands what it means to call the Bible the word of God, then he will also understand that the divine origin of the Bible carries with it certain implications, one of which is that the Bible is a divine communication from God to man, which is couched in language in such a way as to be understood by all men who approach it (cf. John 8:32).

Because premise two of argument #3 (chapter 9-B) is true (see previous discussion, pp. 91ff), premise one of this argument is true. This paves the way for the next premise, premise two of this argument, which simply states that the Bible is the word of God, thus affirming the antecedent of premise one. The proof is as follows:

Argument #3-A

(1) BE > (G v -G) (see discussion to follow)
(2) BE (obvious)
(3) (G v -G) (1, 2 Modus Ponens)
(4) -G > [BM(-I) v GM(-I)] (obvious)
(5) -[BM(-I)] (obvious)
(6) -[GM(-I)] (obvious)
(7) [-BM(-I) . -GM(-I)] (5, 6 Conjunction)
(8) -[BM(-I) v GM(-I)] (7, DeMorgan's Theorem)
(9) - -G (4, 8 Modus Tollens)[13]
(10) G (9, Double Negation)

Argument #3-A, presented above, has as its conclusion the proposition "God is the author if the Bible." The argument in symbolic terms (BE = the Bible exists, G = God authored the Bible, BM(-I) = the Bible was authored by uninspired bad men, GM(-I) = the Bible was authored by uninspired good men) reads as follows:

(1) If the Bible exists, then either God authored the Bible or God did not author the Bible.
(2) The Bible exists.
(3) Therefore, either God authored the Bible or God did not author the Bible.
(4) If God did not author the Bible, then either uninspired bad men wrote the Bible or uninspired good

men wrote the Bible.
(5) Uninspired bad men did not write the Bible.
(6) Uninspired good men did not write the Bible.
(7) Therefore, neither uninspired bad men nor uninspired good men wrote the Bible.
(8) Therefore, it is false to say that the Bible was written by either uninspired bad men or uninspired good men.
(9) It is not the case, therefore, that the Bible was not authored by God.
(10) God, therefore, authored the Bible.

The argument, though lengthy, is most simplistic. Premise one simply affirms that as a consequent of the Bible's existence, either God did or did not author the Bible. The truthfulness of that premise is quite obvious. This premise could very well have been worded in such a way as to say that the Bible's existence implied that either man did or did not write the Bible. If this procedure were adopted, the initial premises would differ, but the conclusion would remain the same.

Premise two simply affirms that the Bible does exist. This, too, is most obvious.

Premise three, by Modus Ponens, affirms that the Bible either is or is not authored by God, another obvious implication.

Premise four then, deals with one of the conjuncts of the consequent in premise three. If God is not the author of the Bible, then man must have authored it, and if man must have authored it, then only uninspired bad men or uninspired good men could have done so, for these are the only possibilities among men.[14]

Premises five and six simply state that neither uninspired bad men nor uninspired good men authored the Bible. This conclusion is reached by examining the characteristics of the Bible. The Bible contains prophecies (e.g., the birth of Christ, the place of his birth, et. al) and the fulfillment of such prophecies. These prophecies and their fulfillments are of such nature that no man, good or bad, could have written

- 126 -

them without inspiration. Thus, premise seven simply conjoins the previous two premises.

Premise eight is logically equivalent to premise seven (via DeMorgan's Theorem), and is the negation of the consequent of premise four.[15] Premise nine, therefore, by Modus Tollens concludes that it is false to say that God did not author the Bible, or as premise ten states, it is true to affirm that God did author the Bible.

The same conclusion, that is that the Bible is the word of God, could be reached by use of a constituent element argument. That argument is summed up by Warren in the following:

> The Bible is the one and only authoritative rule of faith and practice. The basic argument in which this conclusion is drawn is as follows: (1) If it is the case that A, that B, that C,...and that T are all true of a candidate being considered as the inspired and authoritative revelation of God to man, then that candidate is the inspired and authoritative revelation of God to man; (2) It is the case that A, that B, that C,...and that T, are all true of the Bible; (3) Therefore, the Bible is the inspired and authoritative revelation of God to man. (In this argument A, B, C,...T all stand for some affirmative propositions regarding some fact about the Bible.) The argument is valid in form (a hypothetical syllogism in which the antecedent of the major premise is affirmed.)[16]

Argument #3, therefore, because it contains true premises (the truth of premise two, that we can know that the Bible is the word of God, having just been demonstrated) and is valid in form, must render a true conclusion. In this case the conclusion is that we can know that the Bible teaches X. Further argumentation will yield the conclusion that we can know all that is necessary for us to know to obtain salvation and to live right in God's sight.

Argument #4

(1) KBWG > KBASE (see discussion)
(2) KBASE > KBTMMDTBS (see discussion)
(3) KBTMMDTBS > DBTMMDTBS (see discussion)
(4) DBTMMDTBS > S (see discussion)
(5) KBWG (cf. arg.#3-A)
(6) KBASE (1, 5 Modus Ponens)
(7) KBTMMDTBS (2, 6 Modus Ponens)
(8) DBTMMDTBS (3, 7 Modus Ponens)
(9) S (4, 8 Modus Ponens)

The immediately preceding argument has as its conclusion the proposition "man can be saved." The argument begins with the conclusion of the previous argument, which proved that the Bible is the word of God, and proceeds to the conclusion mentioned above. The argument, as presented in symbolic form (KBWG = we can know that the Bible is the word of God, KBASE = we can know that the Bible is all sufficient epistemologically, KBTMMDTBS = we can **know** that the Bible teaches what man must do to be saved, DBTMMDTBS = we can **do** what the Bible teaches man must do to be saved, S = we can be saved) would read as follows:
 (1) If we can know that the Bible is the word of God, then we can know that the Bible is all sufficient epistemologically.
 (2) If we can know that the Bible is all sufficient epistemologically, then we can know that the Bible teaches what man must do to be saved.
 (3) If we can **know** that the Bible teaches what man must do to be saved, then we can **do** what the Bible teaches man must do to be saved.

(4) If we can do what the Bible teaches man must do to be saved, then we can be saved.
(5) We can know that the Bible is the word of God.
(6) Therefore, we can know that the Bible is all sufficient epistemologically.
(7) We can **know**, therefore, what the Bible teaches man must do to be saved.
(8) We can, therefore, **do** what the Bible teaches man must do to be saved.
(9) Man, then, can be saved.

The argument is valid in form, consisting of several hypothetical syllogisms of which the antecedent is repeatedly affirmed, thus yielding the truthfulness of the consequent (by Modus Ponens). The premises are true. The conclusion, therefore, is also true: Man can be saved.

Premise one states: If we can know that the Bible is the word of God, then we can know that the Bible is all sufficient epistemologically. This premise, though true, is in need of explanation. Of the previous arguments given, we noted two which yielded as their conclusion the proposition "we can know that the Bible is the word of God."

The first of those arguments began with the existence of the Bible and reasoned, through the use of a disjunctive syllogism, to the conclusion that God authored the Bible. The second argument, though not presented in symbolic form contained (in word form) the summary of a constituent element argument which would demonstrate that the Bible is the word of God. That summary argument, should it be put into symbolic form and all its premises explained, would contain one premise which affirmed that the Bible is all sufficient epistemologically. This is simply to say that the Bible provides all that needs to be known with respect to every area of knowledge that relates to the salvation of man.

The Bible, therefore, contains all that we need to know about God (e.g., his existence, his attributes, et. al.), Jesus Christ (e.g., his deity, his humanity, his vicarious atonement, et. al.), man (e.g., created in the image of God, his fall into sin, his need for redemption, et. al.), and salvation (e.g., God's role, Christ's role, man's role, et. al.). It can be readily seen, then, that if the Bible is indeed the word of God, then it will be all sufficient epistemologically. (cf. II Timothy 3:14ff; II Peter 1:3-4; et. al.)

The second premise of argument #4 states: If we can know that the Bible is all sufficient epistemologically, then we can know that the Bible teaches what man must do to be saved. The truthfulness of this premise is self-evident. If the Bible is all sufficient epistemologically, as described above, then the Bible will certainly contain the necessary information that needs to be known for the salvation of man.

The third premise of argument #4 states: If we can know that the Bible teaches what man must do to be saved, then we can do what the Bible teaches man must do to be saved. This, too, is axiomatic. If God, who is infinite in all respects, including love, reveals unto us his will so that we might be pleasing in his sight, then it is obvious that the will of God might not only be understood, but also obeyed. We can, therefore, do that which God requires us to do in order to obtain salvation.

Premise four of argument #4 states: If we can do what the Bible teaches must be done by man in order to be saved, then we can be saved. Once again, this premise, like the rest, is self-evident. If God has revealed his will to us, and if we can know and understand his will, and if we can obey his will, then we can be what God would have us to be...saved.

Premise five simply states that we can know that the Bible is the word of God. Argumentation previously presented demonstrated the truthfulness of this conclusion. Because of this affirmation, it is possible to conclude several other propositions.

First, if the Bible is the word of God (and it is), then the Bible is all sufficient epistemologically (as previously explained). This follows by Modus Ponens.

Second, if the Bible is all sufficient epistemologically (as premise six concludes), then we can know that the Bible teaches what man must do to be saved. This, too, follows by Modus Ponens.

Third, if we can know that the Bible teaches what man must do to be saved (as previously indicated), then we can do what the Bible teaches man must do to be saved. This, like the previous conclusions, follows by Modus Ponens.

Finally, if we can do what the Bible says man must do to be saved, then we can be saved. This conclusion follows by Modus Ponens, as did the rest.

From the initial affirmation of the antecedent in premise one (i.e., premise five: "we can know that the Bible is the word of God"), we came (logically) to conclude the remaining propositions, ending with "man can be saved."

This argument is intricately related to the thesis of this work. Effort has been made to demonstrate that "we can know that the Bible teaches X, where X is any true Bible proposition." This last argument referred specifically to salvation, a topic about which the Bible speaks. In the previous argument, "what man must **know** to be saved," "what man must **do** to be saved," and "salvation" itself were all substitutes for X, or should I say that X has functioned all along for these (and other) propositions which are actually taught in the Bible as true. If we can know these specifics, which we have just demonstrated can be known, then the general statement "we can know that the Bible teaches X, where X is any true Bible proposition" is indeed a true statement/proposition. Proving this has been the objective of this work.

<u>If we can know that the Bible teaches X, where X is any true Bible proposition, then we can know everything that we need to know in order to become a Christian, and everything that we need to know in order to remain a faithful Christian in God's sight. In brief, we can learn all that we need to know in order</u>

to be saved here, and hereafter.

---

1. Thomas B. Warren, "The Bible Is God's Word—The Meaning Of And Basic Argument For This Claim," The Inspiration And Authority Of The Bible, p. 2

2. For a discussion of the disjunctive syllogism see Copi, Introduction To Logic, pp. 249ff.

3. cf. John Baillie, Our Knowledge Of God (New York: Charles Scribner's Sons, 1959) for a thorough discussion of this position.

4. John Hick, "Introduction," The Existence Of God ed. by John Hick (New York: Macmillan Publishing Co., Inc., 1964), p. 14

5. I am indebted to Professor William Collins' class "Critique of Contemporary Religious Epistemology," Tennessee Graduate School of Christian Doctrine and Apologetics, Spring 1980 for an introduction to the concepts of both Baillie and Hick.

6. J.D. Thomas, "Knowing God's Will," in The Living And Abiding Word—1979 Freed-Hardeman Lectures ed. William Woodson (Henderson, Tn.: Freed-Hardeman College, 1979), pp. 218-219

7. Ibid., p. 219

8. Clark Pinnock, Biblical Revelation, pp. 33-34

9. Alexander Campbell, Christianity Restored: "The Principle Extras Of The Millennial Harbinger, Revised And Corrected", pp. 22-23

10. Thomas Warren, "Which 'Issues' Before Us Are Most Crucial?," SPIRITUAL SWORD, ed. Thomas Warren,

July 1977, p. 12

11. The wording of argument #2 is identical in thought, but is different in that it reflects Bible knowledge as opposed to general knowledge.

12. It is important to note that the very act of questioning whether or not knowledge is possible is, in itself, tantamount to affirming that knowledge is, indeed, possible. In other words, the very question presupposes that knowledge is possible.

13. This argument is adapted from that which is presented by Roy Deaver in "The Deity Of Christ," BIBLICAL NOTES, ed. Roy Deaver, August, 1980, pp. 51-62

14. Deaver included "inspired" men as a possibility, but if men were "inspired" this would imply God as the source. Thus, it is assumed that all men are uninspired and either good or bad.

15. For further information on DeMorgan's Theorem (or any argument form or logical equivalence) see Copi, Introduction To Logic, or any other standard logic text.

16. Thomas B. Warren, "The Bible Is Inspired And Authoritative - Our Basic Argument," SPIRITUAL SWORD, ed. Thomas B. Warren, January 1970, p. 2

CHAPTER ELEVEN:

OBJECTIONS TO THE THESIS CONSIDERED

In the previous chapter (cf. p.114) a brief allusion was made to criticisms of propositional revelation, the mode of communication defended in conjunction with the basic thesis of this work. It is only fair, therefore, to consider in more detail possible objections that might be lodged against this thesis. Though the following list of objections is not exhaustive, it is hoped that it is representative of the different types of arguments that might be posed in objection to this work.[1]

Objection #1

Let us suppose that it is simply stated that the thesis of this work is in error. In other words, let us suppose that someone sought to affirm the following proposition: **We cannot know what the Bible teaches about X, where X is any true Bible proposition.** This position is an extreme agnostic position. It **does not affirm** that we **can know SOME elements** of Bible teaching but that we **cannot know other elements.** Rather, it **affirms that we cannot know ANY elements of Bible teaching at all.**

In response to this objection, consider the following argument which shows the consequences of objection #1:

(1) -KBTX > -KBWG (see discussion to follow)
(2) -KBWG > -GRWMMDTBS (obvious)
(3) -GRWMMDTBS > -GI(B v P v K) (obvious)
(4) -GI(B v P v K) > -GI (obvious)
(5) -GI > -GE (obvious)
(6) -KBTX (affirmed by hermeneutical agnostic)
(7) -KBWG (1, 6 Modus Ponens)

- 134 -

(8) -GRWMMDTBS (2, 7 Modus Ponens)
(9) -GI(B v P v K) (3, 8 Modus Ponens)
(10) -GI (4, 9 Modus Ponens)
(11) -GE (5, 10 Modus Ponens)

The above argument, given in symbolic terms (Key: -KBTX = we cannot know that the Bible teaches X, where X is any true Bible proposition, -KBWG = we cannot know that the Bible is the word of God, -GRWMMDTBS = God has not revealed what man must do to be saved, -GI(B v P v K) = God is not infinite in either benevolence or power or knowledge, -GI = God is not infinite, -GE = God does not exist), is read as follows:

(1) If we cannot know that the Bible teaches X, where X is any true Bible proposition, then we cannot know that the Bible is the word of God.

(2) If we cannot know that the Bible is the word of God, then God has not revealed what man must do to be saved.

(3) If God has not revealed what man must do to be saved, then God is not infinite in either benevolence or power or knowledge.

(4) If God is not infinite in either benevolence or power or knowledge, then God is not infinite.

(5) If God is not infinite, then God does not exist.

(6) We cannot know that the Bible teaches X, where X is any true Bible proposition.

(7) Therefore, we cannot know that the Bible is the word of God.

(8) God, therefore, has not revealed what man must do to be saved.

(9) God, then, is not infinite in either benevolence or power or knowledge.

(10) God is not infinite.

(11) Thus, God does not exist.

This argument has as its key premise the assumption that the Bible cannot be understood (i.e., premise six). This premise is representative of the agnostic position in Biblical hermeneutics. If this position is maintained, then the consequences of the above argument logically follow.

The first premise of the preceding argument is logically equivalent to the first premise of argument #3 (chapter 10) by the logical move of transposition. It is also identical to premise two in argument #3 (chapter 9-B) [cf. the discussion of these premises, pp. 89ff and 124ff]. This premise (-KBTX > -KBWG) is in need of explanation.

It says: If we cannot know that the Bible teaches X, where X is any true Bible proposition, then we cannot know that the Bible is the word of God. Its meaning, quite simply, is this: In order to know that the Bible is the word of God, one must be able to know certain things about the Bible which would demand such a conclusion.

If, however, it is impossible to know those specific tenets about the Bible which would yield the conclusion that the Bible is the word of God, then quite obviously it would not be possible to know whether or not it really is God's word. For example, we could not know of predictive prophecies and their fulfillments if the Bible were not subject to knowledge. We could not know that the Bible was historically, geographically, epistemologically, and soteriologically correct if we could not know what the Bible teaches about any given subject. If these things be true, as hermeneutical agnosticism presumes they are, then we could not know the Bible to be God's word.

The second premise, then, continues the argument by noting further consequences related to the conclusion of the first premise. If we cannot know that the Bible is the word of God, then God has not revealed what man must do to be saved. Furthermore, as a corollary to this premise (though not mentioned in the symbolic argumentation previously presented), if God has not revealed what man must do to be saved, then it reasonably follows that man could not know what to do to be saved. This premise (i.e., premise two) assumes, of course, that the Bible, if it is the word of God, is

God's **sole revelation to man.** Thus, if the Bible is not God's word, then there exists no other revelation of God to man. Man could not, then, know what he needed to do to be saved.

Premise three states: If God has not revealed what man must do to be saved, then God is not infinite in either benevolence or power or knowledge. Assuming for the moment that God does exist, and that God has not revealed himself, we must conclude one of the following:

(1) Either God exists and did not reveal what man must do to be saved because he is less than infinite in benevolence, that is to say that God does not love man enough to reveal what man must do to be saved; or

(2) God exists and did not reveal what man must do to be saved because he is less than infinite in power, which is to say that God was simply unable to reveal what man must do to be saved; or

(3) God exists and did not reveal what man must do to be saved because he is less than infinite in knowledge, which simply means that God did not reveal what man must do to be saved because God did not know how to accomplish this feat.

If any of the above three propositions is true, then God has not revealed his will to man, and is, therefore, in some way, deficient.

The fourth premise builds upon the previous premise. It says: If God is not infinite in either benevolence or power or knowledge, then God is not infinite. This is most obvious. If God lacked the attribute of infinity in any aspect of his nature, not only would he be less than infinite in that respect, but his entire nature would thus be characterized as less than infinite, or finite.

The fifth premise yields the final premise in the chain of hypothetical syllogisms. It states: If God is not infinite, then God does not exist. We must note that for the purposes of this work we have assumed that God not only exists, but that God is also infinite in all of his attributes. It **necessarily** follows from

- 137 -

God's existence that God must be infinite. God's existence is non-contingent; God is totally self-sustaining. His very nature is to exist. To contend, then, that God is lacking in some aspect of his nature, is to contend that he is less than infinite in that respect, and thus less than infinite overall. Though many philosophers and theologians are willing to admit that it is possible for a finite "God" to exist, a finite "God" is not the God of Biblical theism.[2]

As mentioned at the beginning of the discussion of this argument, the key premise is premise six. That premise simply states that we cannot know that the Bible teaches X, where X is any true Bible proposition. The truthfulness of this premise is assumed for the purposes of this argument because this premise accurately represents the contention of those who maintain agnosticism in Biblical hermeneutics. Given the truthfulness of this premise, the remaining consequences necessarily follow:

(1) We cannot know that the Bible is the word of God (premise seven),

(2) God has not revealed what man must do to be saved [Thus, man cannot know what he must do to be saved. (premise eight)],

(3) God is not infinite in either benevolence or power or knowledge (premise nine),

(4) God is not infinite (premise ten), and

(5) God does not exist (premise eleven).

The ultimate consequence of hermeneutical agnosticism is that God, the infinite God of the Bible, does not exist. It must be remembered, however, that the existence of the infinite God of the Bible has been previously demonstrated (cf. pp. 97ff). The conclusion, therefore, of the previous argument based upon an objection made to this thesis, must be false. If we chose to carry out that argument in symbolic terms, we would show, by a series of Modus Tollens arguments, that premises six through ten were also false. Premise six, you will recall, is the position of the agnostic with regard to Biblical interpretation.

That premise, if proven to be false, results in the downfall of the agnostic position in Biblical hermeneutics. Its assumption was only made in the previous argument in order to show the consequences of this position. When the consequences are shown to be false, we can only conclude that the assumption, too, must be false.

This is, perhaps, one of the most important, yet frequently overlooked mistakes made in philosophy and religion. Many have blindly sought to affirm positions without giving due consideration to the implications (consequences) of those positions. The following remarks by D. Elton Trueblood with respect to this important facet of logic cannot be emphasized enough:

> What are the implications which follow if the original position is affirmed? Often these implications are found to be truly alarming. If the implications of the idea are found to be patently false, ridiculous, or self-contradictory, then the original idea must be abandoned, and we must start all over again. .... In short, the denial of the consequent leads inevitably to the denial of the antecedent. The basic rule of philosophy, is therefore <u>It is not intellectually honest to hold a position after it is known that the position leads inevitably to other positions which are recognized as false</u>. The respect for honesty involves, thus, the respect for consistency. This presumably is accepted by all; if it is not accepted, intelligent discourse may as well come to an end.³

In response to the first objection lodged against the thesis of this work, we must conclude that, due to its insurmountable negative implications, the objection must be overturned.

Objection #2

A second objection that might be lodged against this thesis deals with the communicative ability of God. Because so much attention has already been devoted to this facet of the problem (cf. pp. 110ff.), only a review will be presented here.

It might be maintained that it is impossible to know that the Bible teaches X, where X is any true Bible proposition, because God is not able to communicate/reveal his will to man. We have already noted, however, that if God cannot communicate (i.e., reveal) his will to man, then God must be deficient in some respect. Either **he does not know how to communicate**, in which case he is less than omniscient; or **he does not want to**, in which case he is less than omnibenevolent; or **he does not have the power to communicate**, in which case he is less than omnipotent.

If any of these possibilities is true, then God is less than infinite not only in that respect, but also in his overall nature. God's finitude, therefore, would make him less than the God of the Bible, and less than the God necessary to account for the existence of all the physical creation. The God of the Bible, therefore, would not exist.

It has already been demonstrated, however, that the God of the Bible does exist. If God does exist, and if he is infinite in all respects (as his necessary existence demands), then there can be no doubt that God is able to communicate/reveal his will to man.[4]

Objection #3

A third objection, which must of necessity be discussed, involves the ubiquitous occurrence of varying interpretations of the Bible. If it is true, as this thesis contends, that the Bible really can be understood and obeyed, they why is it the case that so many different interpretations exist? There are a number of reasons for this problem, some of which are set forth here:

(1) One reason why so many different interpretations of specific Bible passages are in existence centers around language. Many people, though well intentioned and sincere, misrepresent the Bible due to ignorance of Biblical languages. Numerous are the misconceptions that have arisen over the Biblical teaching with respect to baptism, for example, because someone did not understand the meaning of the term **baptizo** as it was used in the first century.[5] This same sort of example could be cited many, many times as it relates to the meaning of the Bible in other areas.

(2) Some different interpretations have occurred due to existing differences in the numerous translations available to the public. Some, in their efforts to maintain a particular doctrine, have used specific translations in defense of their positions, without regard to whether or not those translations accurately represent the teaching of the Greek New Testament. A.T. Robertson, long time student of Biblical Greek, has noted the following with respect to this pervasive problem: "The Greek New Testament is the New Testament. All else is translation."[6]

(3) Many varying interpretations develop due to misconceptions about the subject being studied. Some might begin a study of a Bible topic with preconceived ideas about something else, which in truth affects the conclusions they reach about the topic under consideration. Calvinism, for example, with its emphasis upon the total hereditary depravity of man, has approached the Bible in such a way as to "color" almost every Bible teaching with respect to the salvation of man.[7]

(4) Some problems in interpretation have come to the fore due to the motives of Bible students. Those who set out with goals that are not in harmony with truth and righteousness have often gone to the Bible to "prove" some pet theory. In these efforts to bolster

false doctrines many passages of the Bible have been twisted to fit already formed conclusions.

(5) Many problems arise when the Bible is viewed in a false manner. Those who maintain that the Bible is simply another book, or uninspired, or laced with contradictory passages, will, of course, develop interpretations of passages that are not in harmony with the overall theme of God's word.

(6) Numerous problems have surfaced because different Bible scholars have maintained that the Bible was never meant to be understood anyway, but rather that it is some deep and dark, mysterious book which can only confuse and frustrate those who seek to search for its true meaning. This position is in direct opposition to the thesis of this work.

(7) Perhaps the greatest number of problems have come from within "Christendom." Those who maintain the purest intentions have often misinterpreted the Bible through ignorance. They quite simply do not have a firm grasp of the most basic hermeneutical principles: Who is the author? To whom was he writing? Why did he write? What is the background of the author and the readers? To what extent, if any, does the historical, geographical, political, economic, religious, or social background affect the passage under consideration? When was this written? These most fundamental principles are frequently overlooked and, as a result, many Bible passages are interpreted to mean something other than that which was intended by God.

(8) Numerous erroneous interpretations arise when the student of the Bible misunderstands the intention of God. The intention of God, perhaps, is **the most important of all principles to keep in mind.** Some have missed this point entirely and have defended erroneous interpretations because they insisted that the intent of the passage could only be understood from some other perspective. Let me explain.

In seeking to understand any given passage in the Bible, the following aspects need to be considered: (1)

what we think the passage means to us today; (2) what the passage **really** means to us today; (3) what we think the passage meant to the original readers/auditors; (4) what the original auditors/readers **really** thought; (5) what we think the speaker/writer intended; (6) what the speaker/writer **really** intended; (7) what we think God intended; and (8) what God **really** intended.

All of these concepts are important, but some of them are not quite as important as others. For example, it is good to have an understanding of what the passage under consideration means to us (#1), but it is possible that our understanding is nowhere near the meaning which the original readers/auditors had. Unfortunately, this is too often the only means taken in approaching the Bible.

In addition to that, we must also note that the understanding of the initial audience (#4) is not always the same as what we think they understood (#3) or what the speaker/writer or God really intended (#6, #8). For example, as we read the epistles which Paul wrote to the church at Thessalonica, it becomes evident that the readers of the first epistle misunderstood some of Paul's teachings, which necessitated the writing of a second epistle to straighten the matter out. To understand the first epistle, therefore, from the standpoint of the Thessalonian brethren would have been insufficient, for they misunderstood Paul's teachings.

Furthermore, in some Bible passages it is not enough to know only the intent of the author/speaker of the passage under consideration. For example, Peter, on the day of Pentecost, said "For this promise is unto you, and to your children, and to all that are afar off, even as many as the Lord our God shall call" (Acts 2:39). If we sought to base our understanding of this verse entirely on Peter's understanding, we would fall short of God's intended meaning. Peter later had to be convinced of the need to evangelize the Gentiles (cf. Acts 10-11), but it is plain that the evangelization of the Gentiles is included within the meaning of this passage in Acts 2. Likewise, the prophets of Old Testament Israel had only incomplete conceptions of their own messages (cf. I Peter 1:10 ff.). To understand Isaiah 2:1-4 only from the perspective of the prophet Isaiah, who lived in the eighth century before Christ, would be most insufficient indeed. Without examining the rest of the Bible's teaching on the subject, we would never have a full meaning of the passage.

An important key, then, to understanding the Bible, is to seek first (i.e., primarily) God's intention...not our personal opinion, not the understanding of the original audience, not the writer's or speaker's thinking. This can only be obtained when all of the Bible is studied, not just portions of the Bible. When our understanding of the passage is based upon God's intended meaning, then we will have achieved what God wants us to achieve. The Bible plainly teaches that we can achieve God's intended meaning (cf. I Corinthians 2:9-13; Ephesians 3:1-5).

(9) Many opposing interpretations are evident merely due to a lack of further Bible study. Many people, in an attempt to teach about God's offer of salvation to man, have gone to John 3:16...and stayed there! Though we must admit that everything God teaches in John 3:16 is true, we must not believe that John 3:16 teaches every truth there is to know about salvation. It is necessary, yes, but it is not sufficient. So many problems arise because Bible students simply do not study **all that the Bible has to say with respect to a given subject.** They seem to want the "answer" they seek in just a sentence or two, but it is not always that easy.

The importance of this principle, that is of studying all that the Bible has to say about a given subject, is seen by examining$_8$ what seems to be a fairly insignificant passage.

On the night in which he was betrayed, Jesus went to the garden of Gethsemane. All four of the gospel narratives refer to this. As we study Mark 14:47 we note: "And one of them that stood by drew a sword, and smote a servant of the high priest, and cut off his ear." If you were teaching somebody about the events that took place on that occasion, and you referred to this passage, you would be examining a passage that taught the truth about the events of that night, but you would not be examining all that the Bible taught on the subject.

In addition to studying Mark's account, we must also notice what else the Bible says about this subject. For instance, Matthew says: "And, behold, one of them which were with Jesus stretched out his hand, and drew his sword, and struck a servant of the high priest's, and smote off his ear" (Matthew 26:51). Matthew adds the following information: (1) The person standing there was one who was "with Jesus" and (2) he used "his sword" to cut off the ear of the high priest's servant.

Upon closer examination, however, we learn that even this is not "all" of the truth. Luke, another of the "gospel" writers states: "When they which were about him saw what would follow, they said unto him, Lord, shall we smite with the sword? And one of them smote the servant of the high priest, and cut off his right ear. And Jesus answered and said, SUFFER YE THIS FAR. And he touched his ear, and healed him." (Luke 22:49-51). From this passage we learn additional information: (1) Those with Jesus first asked about using swords. (2) It was the right ear of the high priest's servant that was cut off. (3) Jesus said "SUFFER YE THIS FAR." And, (4) Jesus touched the ear of the servant and healed him. Had we consulted only Mark or Matthew, or even Mark **and** Matthew, we would have missed these bits of additional information. Only Luke stresses these facts. Therefore, to have ignored what Luke said would be tantamount to studying only **PART** of the truth.

But we are not finished yet, for there exists one more account of this event. John the apostle informs us: "Then Simon Peter having a sword drew it, and smote the high priest's servant, and cut off his right ear. The servant's name was Malchus. . . . . One of the servants of the high priest, being his kinsman whose ear Peter cut off, saith, Did I not see thee in the garden with him?" (John 18:10, 26). From this passage we learn the final bits of information: (1) It was Simon Peter who drew his sword and cut off the ear of the high priest's servant. (2) The name of the servant was Malchus, and (3) one of his (i.e., Malchus') relatives was present on the occasion.

When, then, did we learn the truth? Did we learn the truth when we studied Mark's account? Yes! But did we learn all of the truth? NO! Did we learn the truth when we studied Matthew's account? Yes! But did we learn all of the truth? NO! Did we learn the truth when we studied Luke's account? Yes! But did we learn all of the truth? NO! Did we learn the truth when we studied John's account? Yes! But did we learn all of the truth from John's account alone? NO! When did we learn all of the truth about this particular incident? We learned all of the truth about this particular incident when **we studied all four of the accounts together.** Everything that we learned up to that point was true, but **it was not all of the truth**!

The great lesson is, of course, that we must study all of the Bible's teaching on any given subject before we can unequivocally state **ALL** of the truth on that subject. This principle applies not only to the example discussed, but rather to all that the Bible teaches. For example, those who seek to learn what the Bible teaches about salvation should take a concordance and search for every New Testament occurrence of the words "save," "saved," "saves," "salvation," as well as **every** other synonymous word and compile a list of those things that are said to contribute to salvation. The list you compile will show that many things contribute to salvation (e.g. faith, hope, repentance, confession, baptism, grace, obedience, et. al.). This, then, is an extremely important principle that is often overlooked as many go about interpreting the Bible.

There are, of course, many other reasons why varying interpretations result. There are many more hermeneutical principles and rules that need to be mastered, but those presented previously are of such a general nature that their inclusion is essential to this work.

It must be noted, however, that varying interpretations do not absolutely necessitate the conclusion that a given passage or subject cannot be understood. The biggest problem comes when the interpretations are directly opposing, but it is entirely conceivable that two different interpretations of a passage are correct if, and only if, they are interpretations of two different aspects of the passage. Let me explain.

We must remember that though we can learn all that God would have us to learn so that we can be all that God would have us to be, there exists much more to learn about any given subject. When the possibilities of the limits of Bible knowledge were previously discussed, it was noted that we can learn and know something about every Bible passage, but that it would be presumptuous to say that we could learn everything there is to know about a Bible passage. God, of course, would know everything that was to be known about a given passage, but we must not assume that what we know about a given passage is all that can be known. It is often the case that Bible students, though having a true knowledge of a passage, learn something new about that passage when it is studied again. It is not necessary to view the new knowledge as being in opposition to what was already learned. Thus, some new interpretation was seen to corroborate a previous interpretation. Both can be true.

In conclusion, to say that different interpretations exist does not necessarily imply that the thesis of this work is false. But, to say that opposing interpretations are both true would, in fact, be a denial of this thesis. The problem lies within the different approaches taken in interpreting the Bible, and not within the Bible itself.

Objection #4

Another possible objection that might be made against this thesis deals with the limits of Bible knowledge. Some have maintained that a claim to know everything that one must know in order to be saved is equivalent to claiming that one must know absolutely everything. This would be, of course, a ridiculous claim, and **it most certainly is NOT the contention of this thesis.**

It is not necessary to know **everything** about any given discipline before one can claim to know **anything** about that particular field. For example, I do not know all that there is to know about physics, but I do know, however, that all matter exists in one of the following three states: solid, liquid, or gas. My lack of total knowledge does not preclude my lack of any knowledge.

The same is true with regard to the limits of Bible knowledge. I do not know, nor claim to know, all that there is to know about the Bible. I do, however, know specific Bible facts about many different subject areas. To say, then, that a claim to any knowledge, is equivalent to a claim of all knowledge, is most preposterous. This thesis in not guilty of such a claim.

Objection #5

The following objection must also be considered: "If the Bible teaches that we cannot know everything, how can we be sure that what we claim it teaches we can know is not in reality a part of that which it really teaches that we cannot know?"

This objection deals with the crux of Biblical epistemology. **If some Bible facts can be known, but** other facts cannot be known, how can we know which are truly knowable and which are not? Furthermore, how can we know that we know what is truly knowable? And, how do we know that what we really need to know is not that which is unknowable? All of these questions have, in effect, been answered through previous argumentation. It will prove beneficial, however, to summarize these arguments in answer to this line of questioning.

First, the Bible makes reference to the limits of knowledge in many places. For example, Jesus, in John 8:32, declared that truth could be known. He did not, however, state that all truth could be known, but rather set the delimitations for the area of truth about which he spoke. The immediate context conclusively demonstrates that the "truth" which Jesus said could be known was that "truth" which was needed to make men free from sin (John 8:32-36).

This posture (i.e., of being able to know all the truth concerning salvation) is reflected in the writings of the apostles and other inspired writers of the New Testament. Paul was concerned that some Christians were "ever learning, and never able to come to the knowledge of the truth" (II Timothy 3:7). He did not mean that they could never know any truth that could be known, but rather, as the text indicates, that some, because of other pursuits, would not know the "truth" with respect to salvation. That "truth" was, indeed, subject to knowledge (I Timothy 4:3).

Peter and John, also apostles, wrote concerning the truth. Peter said that souls were purified in "obeying the truth" (I Peter 1:22) and that it was possible to be "established in the present truth" (II Peter 1:12). Each of these passages indicates that "truth," as it relates to salvation, can be known.

John, too, makes numerous references to truth and knowledge in his writings. In I John 2:21 he said: "I have not written unto you because ye know not the truth, but because ye know it..." In his second epistle he commended the children of the elect lady because "they...have known the truth" (II John 1).

Second, the Bible does refer to some topics as being beyond the knowledge of man. Perhaps the most referred to verse in this respect is Deuteronomy 29:29 which says: "The secret things belong unto the Lord our God: but those things which are revealed belong unto us and to our children for ever, that we may do all the words of this law." Note that this verse teaches that there are some things that belong only to God, **but it also teaches that those things which are revealed are revealed so that we may "do all the words of this law."** Needless to say, **those things cannot be done unless we can understand what they are in the first place.** This passage, then, though it teaches that we cannot know some things, also teaches that we <u>can know</u> other things.

It is important to distinguish between the types of subjects which are beyond our knowledge: (1) There are those elements of Bible teaching that we do not presently know, but which we may learn through further study (II Peter 2:2; 3:18). (2) There are those facets of Bible teaching that we do not presently comprehend, but which we will comprehend in eternity (I John 3:1-2). (3) There are those Bible teachings which we do not presently understand, and which we will never fully understand (Romans 11:33-36; Ephesians 3:8; Psalm 145:3; Job 5:9; Isaiah 40:28; Ecclesiastes 3:11; 8:17; et. al.).

In conclusion, then, the Bible teaches (1) that the truth necessary for the salvation of man can be known and (2) that there are certain areas of knowledge that are presently beyond the grasp of human knowledge. <u>IT IS IMPORTANT TO NOTE, HOWEVER, THAT THE BIBLE NEVER REPRESENTS ANY KNOWLEDGE OF TRUTH WHICH IS NECESSARY FOR THE SALVATION OF MAN AS BEING BEYOND HUMAN ATTAINMENT.</u> We can know, therefore, that knowledge is attainable, that knowledge about salvation is attainable, that we can know that we know, and that we can know that there are some things that we do not know. **The Bible** clearly sets forth the limitations of knowledge.

Objection #6

The sixth objection might be best expressed this way: "Is there not any middle ground with reference to what we can and cannot know?"

It is true that there exist some specific areas where middle ground not only exists, but where it is the preferred position. Such is not the case in epistemology. Everything is either known or unknown, knowable or unknowable. True, there are many things that we do not know very much about, but the little we do know about them is still known. Epistemology is, in this respect, an either/or matter.

Agnosticism has approached epistemology in two ways. First, some proponents of agnosticism have maintained that no decision is presently available due to insufficient information. Second, some advocates of agnosticism have contended that no decision can be made because the specific subject under consideration is simply unknowable.

The first position can properly reflect a real and existing situation. There might be some decisions with respect to given subjects that are presently suspended due to a lack of information. This is not to say, however, that such a decision can never be made. The second situation, though, maintains a total suspension of decision making, for this position maintains that the subject under consideration is, in actuality, unknowable. This would be quite alright if, indeed, the subject were beyond the limits of human cognition, but when the subject is within the reach of human knowledge, such a position is completely without merit.

Understanding the Bible, therefore, is, to a very great extent, an either/or matter. **EITHER** the Bible is the word of God, **OR** the Bible is not the word of God. **EITHER** God has communicated to man through the

Bible in such a way that his will can be understood, **OR** God has not communicated in such fashion. **EITHER** man has the ability to understand that communication to the extent that he can be obedient to the will of the Lord, **OR** man does not have such an ability. There exists no middle ground in these situations.

This work has demonstrably maintained that the agnostic position which denies the possibility of all knowledge is untenable. Furthermore, this work has demonstrated that agnosticism in Biblical hermeneutics is false as a general Biblical epistemological position. It is also false as a specific epistemological position concerning those subject areas that are crucial to the salvation of the souls of men. More specifically, this thesis has amply demonstrated that one can know all that the Bible teaches can be known with respect to what a person must believe and obey concerning salvation.

---

1. Future editions of this work will, no doubt, take into consideration those criticisms that come to the fore as a result of the publication of this work.

2. For an example of a philosopher admitting the possible existence of a finite "God," cf. Wallace I. Matson, The Existence Of God (Ithaca, N.Y.: Cornell University Press, 1965), pp. 136-137

3. D. Elton Trueblood, General Philosophy (Grand Rapids: Baker Book House, 1963), pp. 8-9

4. See the previous section referred to above where this subject is discussed more fully.

5. cf. Jay E. Adams, The Meaning And Mode Of Baptism (Phillipsburg, N.J.: Presbyterian and Reformed Publishing Co., 1975. Adams not only contends that

"pouring" is an acceptable "mode" of baptism, he also goes so ridiculously far as to affirm that "immersion" is an unacceptable "mode."

6. A.T. Robertson, A Grammar Of The New Testament In The Light Of Historical Research (Nashville: Broadman Press, 4th ed., 1923), p. xix

7. For a discussion of other things that hinder interpretation, cf. D.R. Dungan, Hermeneutics (Delight, Ark.: Gospel Light Publishing Company, n.d.), pp. 33 ff.

8. Note: All of the Bible is important, but not all passages are directly involved in teaching what one needs to learn, know, obey, and teach to be saved.

CHAPTER TWELVE: PRACTICAL APPLICATIONS

It is, without a doubt, important to understand the principles set forth in conjunction with the thesis of this work and its defense. It is possible, however, that someone might grasp the core of the argumentation and, nonetheless, fail to understand how such applies on a practical basis. To this present dilemma we shall direct the focus of this chapter.

If it is true that we can understand all that God would have us to understand so that we might obtain salvation, that is, if the thesis of this work is true, then how does this truth affect the student of the Bible as he reads and seeks to implement Bible truths in his life? Can he be sure that it is actually possible to know and do what God expects of him?

To answer these questions we need only turn to the Bible and examine its teachings.[1] When such an examination is concluded, we note at least the following four principles and their implications, which demand the conclusion that the Bible is, indeed, subject to human understanding.[2]

God Demands That Truth Be Taught

God has always expected man to teach the truth—nothing more—nothing less. This fundamental facet is evident throughout the Bible. Jesus the Christ, the Son of the living God, was the embodiment of truth (John 1:14; 14:6). Truth came by him (John 1:17). He spoke only the truth (John 8:40, 45-46; 16:7). He expected people to believe, obey, and be sanctified by the truth (John 3:21; 8:32, 46; 17:17, 19).

In like manner, Paul, an apostle of Christ, taught truth wherever he went (Romans 9:1; II Corinthians 2:14; 12:6). James admonished his readers not to lie nor err from the truth (James 3:14; 5:19). Peter taught that our souls were purified by obedience to the truth

(I Peter 1:22) and that Christians were to be established in truth (II Peter 1:12). John, in his three epistles, constantly admonished Christians to walk consistent with the truth (I John 1:6, 8, 2:4, 21; 3:18; II John 1-4; III John 4, 8).

Those who sought to follow Christ were encouraged to believe the truth (John 8:32; Ephesians 1:13) and were warned of the consequences if they did not believe it (John 8:24; II Thessalonians 2:10-12). They were exhorted to speak the truth (Ephesians 4:15, 25), walk in truth (III John 4), obey the truth (Romans 2:8; Galatians 3:1; 5:7; I Peter 1:22), and rightly divide (or "handling aright," ASV) the word of truth (II Timothy 2:15).

If Christ and his apostles taught the truth, and expected their hearers to understand it, believe it, and obey it, does this not entail that we, too, can understand it, believe it, and obey it today? The very concept of truth itself demands that understanding it is possible, else how would we know what truth is, and what is true and what is not? From this perspective we can see that God intended for the Bible to be understood.

God Demands That Error Be Refuted

Implicit within God's demand that truth be taught is the concomitant demand that error be refuted. It is, as a matter of fact, impossible to properly and fully teach truth without engaging in a refutation of error, for the teaching of truth is, prima facie, in opposition to the teaching of error. Every proclamation of truth is, therefore, an effort to combat error.

We must not conclude, however, that in preaching the truth in a "positive" manner, we thus fulfill our obligation to stand against error. Though the teaching of truth necessarily includes a refutation of error, such is merely a <u>general</u> refutation. Error must often be refuted in a <u>specific</u>, "negative" manner. Again, we turn to the teaching of Christ and his disciples for examples of this principle.

We have already noted that Christ was the epitome of a teacher of truth, and, as such, necessarily taught **generally** against error through his teachings. More specifically, however, we note that **Christ was often more direct** in his efforts to combat error. We note, for example, the following instances of Jesus' specific refutation of error:

(1) Jesus spoke directly against the misinterpretations of Satan (Matthew 4:1-11);

(2) He openly confronted the scribes when they questioned his healing of the paralytic (Matthew 9:1ff; Mark 2:3; Luke 5:18);

(3) He dealt face to face with those Pharisees that questioned his, and his disciples', actions on the Sabbath (Matthew 12:1ff; Mark 2:23ff; Luke 6:1ff);

(4) He carefully pointed out the inconsistencies of the Pharisees when they accused him of doing the work of Beelzebub (Matthew 12:22ff);

(5) He plainly declared the scribes and Pharisees guilty of transgressing the commands of God by their traditions (Matthew 15:1ff; Mark 7:1ff);

(6) He rebuked his disciples for their lack of faith (Matthew 8:26; 14:31; 16:8; 17:17);

(7) He chastised impetuous Peter (Matthew 16:22ff);

(8) And, in perhaps his most notable direct confrontation, Jesus referred to the Pharisees, Herodians, and scribes as hypocrites (Matthew 22:18; 23:13-15, 23, 25, 27-29), fools and blind guides (Matthew 23:16-17, 19, 24, 26), white-washed sepulchres full of dead men's bones (Matthew 23:27), serpents, and a generation of vipers (Matthew 23:33). Certainly, a more forceful and direct refutation of error cannot be found than this!

Furthermore, the apostles and disciples of Jesus were called upon to make specific condemnations of sin and sinners. Peter, in his sermon delivered on Pentecost, openly accused the Jews in his listening audience of crucifying the Christ (Acts 2:22ff; cf. 3:14ff; 4:10). He spoke directly to Ananias and Sapphira and accused them of lying to the Lord and to the Holy Spirit (Acts 5:3-4, 8-9).

Stephen, in his address before the high priest and council, openly accused them of being stiffnecked (i.e. rebellious) and uncircumcised (i.e. unwilling to submit to the will of God), persecutors, betrayers, and murderers (Acts 7:51-52).

Paul, in addition to writing numerous epistles to churches to deal with their shortcomings, often mentioned individuals who were involved in sin by name (cf. Demas-II Timothy 4:10; Hymeneus, Alexander, Philetus-I Timothy 1:20; II Timothy 2:17). He even rebuked his fellow apostle Peter to his face when he (i.e. Peter) withdrew from the Gentile Christians and showed partiality to the Jewish Christians (Galatians 2:11ff).

These, and numerous other examples, demonstrate that God expects man to stand against error. But, it is impossible to stand against it unless man has the capacity to know what error is. Thus, man must have the ability to understand the Bible to the extent that he can recognize error and refute it when necessary.

Truth and Error Are Distinguishable

The Bible not only teaches that God expects truth to be taught and error to be refuted, but it also teaches that man has the ability to distinguish between truth and error. This principle is a corollary to the ones just discussed in that the command to teach only the truth implies that it is possible to teach something other than the truth (and that such is not pleasing to God), and that the command to refute error involves the ability to recognize it for what it is (i.e., as error and not as truth) as well as refute it. Both of these demands, then, carry with them the implicit teaching that man has the ability to distinguish between right and wrong.

Man is always presented with a choice; he may do that which is right, or that which is wrong. Moses, almost 3500 years ago, said:

> Behold, I set before you this day a blessing and a curse; A blessing, if ye obey the commandments of the Lord your God, which I command you this day: And a curse, if ye will not obey the commandments of the Lord your God, but turn aside out of the way which I command you this day, to go after other gods, which ye have not known. (Deuteronomy 11:26-28)

God, through Moses, not only presented the children of Israel with a choice, but, at the same time informed them of the consequences of each of the alternatives. In addition to that, God told the children of Israel which of the choices was pleasing to him. Note the following passage which demonstrates this truth:

> For this commandment which I command thee this day, it is not hidden from thee, neither is it far off. It is not in heaven, that thou shouldest say, Who shall go up for us to heaven, and bring it unto us, that we may hear it, and do it? Neither is it beyond the sea, that thou shouldest say, Who shall go over the sea for us, and bring it unto us, that we may hear it, and do it? But the word is very nigh unto thee, in thy mouth, and in thy heart, that thou mayest do it. See, I have set before thee this day life and good, and death and evil:. . . .I call heaven and earth to record this day against you, that I have set before you life and death, blessing and cursing: therefore choose life, that both thou and

thy seed may live:... (Deuteronomy 30:11-15, 19)

The immediately preceding passages affirm that God: (1) expects man to be able to know the difference between right and wrong; (2) expects man to make a choice between right and wrong; (3) presents the consequences of each choice; (4) directs man to make the proper choice; and (5) presents the choices in such a way as to make them abundantly clear and easy to understand for all men.

It is quite clear, therefore, that the Lord's expectation for man to be able to distinguish between truth and error in religious matters necessarily demands that man be able to understand the teachings of the Bible. To affirm otherwise is to affirm that man cannot understand the Bible, but that the Lord expects him to do so anyway. Such could not be a more telling inconsistency.

God Expects Obedience To Truth

The final principle to be discussed is one which ultimately follows from the previous three. God not only wants man to discern between truth and error, defend the truth, and refute error, he also wants, and expects, man to obey him.

Generally speaking, obedience to the will of God has been classified in the following manner: (1) We must do that which God has authorized/commanded us to do, and (2) we must refrain from doing that which God has not authorized/commanded. Thus, failure to do what God has authorized/commanded is deemed a "sin of omission," and doing that which God has not authorized/commanded as a "sin of commission."

The Bible is replete with explicit statements which place upon the reader the obligation of obeying God's will by doing that which God has authorized/commanded us to do. Only a sampling is presented here:

(1) "...do good unto all men, especially unto them who are of the household of faith." (Galatians 6:10)

(2) "...Repent, and be baptized every one of you in the name of Jesus Christ for the remission of sins, and ye shall receive the gift of the Holy Ghost." (Acts 2:38)

(3) "Husbands, love your wives, even as Christ also loved the church and gave himself for it;..." (Ephesians 5:25)

(4) "Pray without ceasing." (I Thessalonians 5:17)

(5) "Submit yourselves to every ordinance of man for the Lord's sake:..." (I Peter 2:13)

In addition to those "positive" commands, the Bible contains those "negative" commands which place upon the reader the responsibility of refraining from certain actions, some of which are noted below:

(1) "Abstain from all appearance of evil." (I Thessalonians 5:22)

(2) "...Thou shalt not commit adultery, Thou shalt not kill, Thou shalt not steal, Thou shalt not bear false witness, Thou shalt not covet;..." (Romans 13:9)

(3) "Speak not evil one of another, brethren." (James 4:11)

(4) "Love not the world, neither the things that are in the world." (I John 2:15)

(5) "Lie not one to another..." (Colossians 3:9)

These commands, both positive and negative, necessarily assume that man has the ability to obey them. But, it is impossible to obey them if impossible to understand them. Thus, it is clear that the giving of such commands implies that man has the ability to understand them.

Every responsibility, therefore, laid upon man by God, through his word, involves both the understanding of that responsibility and the performance of such. Of the more than 31,000 verses in the Bible there are thousands that place such obligation upon man. Each of these passages demand that we have the ability to understand and obey them.

Summary

From the four preceding principles we must conclude that God intended for man to be able to understand the Bible. Every possible classification of Bible knowledge will naturally fall into one, or more, of these four categories. Every passage calls upon the reader to: (1) recognize and defend truth, and/or (2) to recognize and refute error, and/or (3) to discern between truth and error, and/or (4) to practice the truth and avoid practicing error. None of these can be accomplished without the ability to understand the word of God.

As we read our Bibles, then, we must recognize these principles. They are practical principles, understandable by all, which demand that we have the ability to understand God's word. It makes no difference what passage we might be seeking to understand; whether it be prophecy, narrative, or history, **if it is necessary for the salvation of our souls, it can be understood.** To that extent, every passage in the Bible teaches some truth, and to that extent, we can understand the truth.

This is made most clear, not only by the principles set forth above, but especially so by the numerous passages in the Bible which explicitly affirm that God's word can be understood. Some of those are cited here:

(1) "All this, said David, the Lord made be understand in writing by his hand upon me, even all the works of this pattern." (I Chronicles 28:19)

(2) "And Ezra the priest brought the law before the congregation both of men and women, and all that could hear with understanding...and he read...before the mean and women, and those that could understand; and the ears of all the people were attentive unto the book of the law. .... and the Levites caused the people to understand the law: ...so they read in the book in the law of God distinctly, and gave the sense, and caused them to understand the reading. .... even to

understand the words of the law." (Nehemiah 8:3-13)

(3) "Teach me, and I will hold my tongue: and cause me to understand wherein I have erred." (Job 6:24)

(4) "Make me to understand the way of thy precepts:..." (Psalm 119:27)

(5) "But he that received seed into the good ground is he that heareth the word, and understandeth it;..." (Matthew 13:23)

(6) "And he called unto the multitude, and said unto them, Hear and understand:..." (Matthew 15:10; Mark 7:14)

(7) "...(whoso readeth, let him understand:)..." (Matthew 24:15; Mark 13:14)

(8) "Then opened he their understanding, that they might understand the scriptures." (Luke 24:45)

(9) "Whereby, when ye read, ye may understand my knowledge in the mystery of Christ..." (Ephesians 3:4)

(10) "Wherefore be ye not unwise, but understanding what the will of the Lord is." (Ephesians 5:17)

These passages, and many others, coupled with the principles discussed earlier, make it plain to see that God intends for his word to be understood. It is imperative that we keep this in mind as we engage in a study of the Bible.

---

1. Some might claim that turning to the Bible to defend the Bible is but to engage in circular reasoning, but such is not necessarily the case. The Bible is autopistic, that is, it is self-authenticating. Its very nature is such that it "speaks" in its own defense.

2. For further study see Thomas B. Warren's, "Can We Really Gain Religious Knowledge?," SPIRITUAL SWORD, ed. Thomas Warren, July 1972, pp.40ff and "'Ye Shall Know The Truth' Of The Bible," in The Bible Versus Liberalism ed. W.A. Bradfield (Nashville: Gospel Advocate, 1972), pp. 427ff.

CHAPTER THIRTEEN: CONCLUSION

It has been the purpose of this work to demonstrate the truthfulness of premise four of the basic argument for Christianity. That premise states that **we can know that the Bible teaches X, where X is any true Bible proposition. More specifically, this writer set out to demonstrate that all that one needed to know in order to be saved, could, indeed, be known.**

In order to complete this goal, the following was accomplished: (1) The problem was stated.

(2) The thesis of this work was stated.

(3) Definitions, presuppositions, and limitations were given.

(4) Examples of the problem were presented.

(5) Argumentation was given which demonstrated that hermeneutical agnosticism was a false position.

(6) Argumentation in defense of this thesis was presented.

(7) Objections to this thesis were considered.

And, (8) some practical applications of the thesis were discussed.

Though this work has not attempted to deal with every conceivable Bible verse that might cause some difficulty in interpretation, principles were set forth which were representative of alleged difficulties in such a way as to include possible objections.

<u>IT IS POSSIBLE, THEREFORE, TO KNOW.</u>
<u>IT IS POSSIBLE TO KNOW THAT GOD EXISTS AND THAT THE BIBLE IS HIS WORD.</u>
<u>IT IS POSSIBLE TO KNOW WHAT THE BIBLE TEACHES ABOUT MANY SUBJECTS.</u>
<u>IT IS POSSIBLE TO KNOW WHAT THE BIBLE TEACHES CONCERNING WHAT MAN MUST DO TO BE SAVED.</u>
<u>ANY BIBLE PASSAGE THAT MUST BE UNDERSTOOD, IN ORDER TO KNOW WHAT MAN MUST DO TO BE SAVED, CAN BE UNDERSTOOD.</u>

THE DIFFICULTY THAT SOME MAY ENCOUNTER DUE TO THE EMOTIONAL DIFFICULTIES SURROUNDING AN ISSUE [E.G., MARRIAGE, DIVORCE, AND REMARRIAGE] DOES NOT WARRANT THE CONCLUSION THAT SUCH TOPICS ARE BEYOND THE REALM OF HUMAN UNDERSTANDING. THEY ARE ONLY INDICATIVE THAT FURTHER STUDY IS NEEDED BY SOME INDIVIDUALS.

THE TRUTH ON THESE MATTERS, AND ALL OTHERS, IF THEY ARE ESSENTIAL TO THE SALVATION OF MAN, CAN BE KNOWN!

SELECTED BIBLIOGRAPHY

Adams, Jay E. **The Meaning And Mode Of Baptism.** Phillipsburg, N.J.: Presbyterian and Reformed Publishing Co., 1975

Baillie, John. **Our Knowledge Of God.** New York: Charles Scribner's Sons, 1959)

Barnett, Joe R. "Throwaway Marriages," **Up Reach**, Batsell Barrett Baxter, ed. May/June 1980, March/April 1981

Beam, Joe. "I Know I'm Right," **Firm Foundation**, Reuel Lemmons, ed. May 12, 1981

Campbell, Alexander. **Christianity Restored: "The Principle Extras Of The Millennial Harbinger, Revised And Corrected"**. Rosemead, California: The Old Paths Book Club, 1959

Cathcart, Robert. **Post Communication: Criticism And Evaluation.** Indianapolis: The Bobbs-Merrill Company, Inc., 1966

Copleston, F.C., Russell, Bertrand. "A Debate On The Existence Of God," **The Existence Of God**, John Hick, ed. New York: Macmillan Publishing Company, Inc., 1964

Copi, Irving M. **Introduction To Logic.** New York: Macmillan Publishing Company, Inc., 5th ed. 1978

Deaver, Mac. "Agnosticism Is Self-Defeating," **Spiritual Sword**, Thomas B. Warren, ed. July 1977

Deaver, Roy. **How To Study The Bible.** Plano, Texas: Biblical Publishing Corporation, 1976

Deaver, Roy. "The Deity Of Christ," **Biblical Notes**, Roy Deaver, ed. August 1980

Dungan, D.R. **Hermeneutics**. Delight, Arkansas: Gospel Light Publishing Company, n.d.

Eddins, Tom. "Can We Really Be Certain?," **Spiritual Sword**, Thomas B. Warren, ed. July 1977

Ehrlich, E.; Flexner, S.B.; Carruth, G.; Hawkins, J.M.; compilers. **Oxford American Dictionary**. New York: Oxford University Press, 1980

Flew, Antony G.N. **Thinking Straight**. Buffalo, New York: Prometheus Books, 1975

Flint, Robert. **Agnosticism**. New York: Charles Scribner's Sons, 1903

Geisler, Norman L.; Nix, William E. **A General Introduction To The Bible**. Chicago: Moody Press, 1968

Hamlyn, D.W. "History Of Epistemology," **The Encyclopedia Of Philosophy**, Paul Edwards, ed. New York: Macmillan Publishing Company, Inc. and The Free Press, 1967

Hick, John. "Introduction," **The Existence Of God**, John Hick, ed. New York: Macmillan Publishing Company, Inc. 1964

Koster, Helmut. "ORTHOTOMEO," **Theological Dictionary Of The New Testament**. Gerhard Kittel, Gerhard Friedrich, eds. Grand Rapids: William B. Eerdmans Publishing Company, 1964-1976

Lamar, J.S. **Organon Of Scripture**. Rosemead, California: The Old Paths Book Club, 1952

Marle, Rene. **Introduction To Hermeneutics.** New York: Herder and Herder, 1967

Matson, Wallace I. **The Existence Of God.** Ithaca, New York: Cornell University Press, 1965

Mickelsen, A. Berkeley. **Interpreting The Bible.** Grand Rapids: William B. Eerdmans Publishing Company, 1963

Milligan, Robert. **Reason And Revelation.** Cincinnati, Ohio: R.W. Carroll and Company, Publishers, 1868, reprinted by Lambert Book House, 1975

Nielsen, Kai. "Agnosticism," **Dictionary of the History of Ideas.** New York: Charles Scribner's Sons, 1973

Pinnock, Clark. **Biblical Revelation.** Chicago: Moody Press, 1971

Ramm, Bernard. **Protestant Biblical Interpretation.** Grand Rapids: Baker Book House, 3rd. ed. rev. 1970

Roberts, J.W. "Expediency And Pattern Authority," **Abilene Christian College Lectures–1960.** Abilene, Texas: Abilene Christian College, 1960

Robertson, A.T. **A Grammar Of The New Testament In The Light Of Historical Research.** Nashville: Broadman Press, 4th ed., 1923

Ruby, Lionel. **Logic: An Introduction.** Chicago: J.B. Lippincott Company, 1960

Schramm, Wilbur. "How Communication Works," **Communication: Concepts And Processes**, Joseph A. Devito, ed. Englewood Cliffs, New

Jersey: Prentice-Hall, Inc.,1976

Shelly, Rubel. **What Shall We Do With The Bible?**. Jonesboro, Arkansas: National Christian Press, 1975

Shelly, Rubel. "Must We Divide?," **Firm Foundation**, Reuel Lemmons, ed. January 6, 1981

Shelly, Rubel. "Follow Up Thoughts On 'Must We Divide?'," **Firm Foundation**, Reuel Lemmons, ed. December 15, 1981

Shelly, Rubel. "The Restoration Of The Liberty Of Opinion," David Lipscomb College Lectureship, June 16, 1981

Shelly, Rubel. "Christ, The Effective Energy For Unity In The Brotherhood," **Christ Our Effective Energy—Eighth Annual Lectureship.** Knoxville, Tennessee: East Tennessee School Of Preaching And Missions, 1982

Terry, Milton S. **Biblical Hermeneutics.** Grand Rapids: Zondervan Publishing House, 4th printing 1976

Thomas, J.D. **Heaven's Window.** Abilene, Texas: Biblical Research Press, 1974

Thomas, J.D. "Knowing God's Will," **The Living And Abiding Word—1979 Freed-Hardeman Lectures**, William Woodson, ed. Henderson, Tennessee: Freed-Hardeman College, 1979

Thompson, Samuel M. **A Modern Philosophy Of Religion.** Chicago: Henry Regnery Company, 1955

Trueblood, E. Elton. **General Philosophy.** Grand Rapids: Baker Book House, 1963

Verderber, Rudolph F. **Communicate!**. Belmont, California: Wadsworth Publishing Company, Inc., 1975

Vincent, M.R. **Word Studies In The New Testament**. McLean, Virginia: MacDonald Publishing Company, n.d.

Warfield, Benjamin B. "Inspiration," **International Standard Bible Encyclopedia**, James Orr, ed. Grand Rapids: William B. Eerdmans Publishing Company, 1956

Warren, Thomas B. "Critique of Atheism," Class Notes-Tennessee Graduate School of Christian Doctrine and Apologetics, Fall 1979

Warren, Thomas B. **When Is An Example Binding?**. Jonesboro, Arkansas: National Christian Press, 1975

Warren, Thomas B. **Have Atheists Proved There Is No God?**. Jonesboro, Arkansas: National Christian Press, 1975

Warren, Thomas B. **Keeping The Lock In Wedlock**. Jonesboro, Arkansas: National Christian Press, 1980

Warren, Thomas B. "The Bible Is God's Word—The Meaning And Basic Argument For This Claim," **The Inspiration And Authority Of The Bible—1971 Bible Lectureship Of Harding Graduate School Or Religion**, W.B. West, Jr., Bill Flatt, Thomas B. Warren, eds. Nashville: Gospel Advocate, 1971

Warren, Thomas B. "Which 'Issues' Before Us Are Most Crucial?," **Spiritual Sword**, Thomas B. Warren, ed. July 1977

Warren, Thomas B. "The Bible is Inspired And Authoritative--Our Basic Argument," **Spiritual Sword,** Thomas B. Warren, ed. January 1970

Warren, Thomas B. "Can We Really Gain Religious Knowledge?," **Spiritual Sword,** Thomas B. Warren ed. July 1972

Warren, Thomas B. "'Ye Shall Know The Truth' Of The Bible," **The Bible Versus Liberalism-1972 Freed-Hardeman College Lectureship,** W.A. Bradfield ed. Nashville: Gospel Advocate, 1972

Wood, Ledger. "Epistemology," **Dictionary Of Philosophy,** Dagobert D. Runes, ed. Totowa, New Jersey: Littlefield, Adams and Company, 1962 ed.

INDEX OF SUBJECTS AND AUTHORS

agnosticism 1, 3, 8
        arguments against 72ff, 83ff, 102ff, 109ff
        definition of 22, 72
        epistemology and 75, 77
        false application of 74
        hermeneutical (see hermeneutical agnosticism)
        implications of 3, 22, 78, 89, 102, 107
        inconsistency of 44, 76, 79
        objective 74
        subjectivism 83
        thesis and 74, 134, 151ff
arguments
        Modus Ponens 13, 45, 77, 81
        Modus Tollens 81
        sound 14
        unsound 43
        valid 13, 44-45, 75
baptism
        necessity of 57
Baillie, John 112
Barnett, Joe 57, 105
Beam, Joe 42-46
Bible 5
        all-sufficiency of 12, 129ff
        authority of 51, 125ff
        definition of 15, 20
        epistemology and 32, 58
        inspiration and 22, 36, 38, 51, 92, 123ff
        role in God's plan 12, 38
        study of 10
        subject to knowledge 13
Campbell, Alexander 117
Cathcart, Robert 24
Christ
        purpose of 10
Christianity
        basic argument for 1, 13
church

        purpose of 10
communication 16
        definition of 24
        God's ability to (see under God)
        conjunction 48
contingency 98
contradiction
        law of 28, 36
        logical 49, 79, 85
criticism, textual 40
Deaver, Roy 9
definitions 7, 14, 19
disjunction 110
epistemology 8, 13, 15, 16, 21-23, 39, 43-45, 51, 59, 72, 83ff, 120ff, 148ff
        assumptions of 36
        Bible's view of 30, 32
        definition of 29
        thesis and 29, 38
excluded middle, law of 28, 36, 121, 151
God
        Bible and 125
        communication and 24, 95, 111, 114, 140
        definition of 19
        existence of 1, 4, 23, 36, 38, 93ff
        finite 5, 19
        infinity of 95
        process 20
        proof of 97ff
Flew, Antony G.N. 59
Flint, Robert 4, 22, 49
hermeneutics 3, 23, 53ff
        definition of 25
        exegesis and 25
        fundamental question of 8
        God's intention and 142ff
        implementation of 71
        necessity of 63, 71
        origin of 65
        possibility of 63

       problems in 134ff
       role of 25, 66, 72
       thesis and 40, 134ff
hermeneutical agnosticism 4, 5, 7, 8, 24, 36
       argumentation against 7, 43, 63, 83ff, 102ff, 109ff
       epistemology and 31
       examples of 7, 14, 55
       implications of 23, 45, 107
Hick, John 112
Huxley, T.H. 1, 72
identity, law of 28, 36
implication 16
inspiration (see Bible) 1
       definition of 21
interpretation 1, 2, 23, 41, 140
knowledge (see epistemology) 29, 43-45,59
       of Bible 13
       limits of 29, 73, 120ff, 148, 149ff
       possibility of 29, 36 , 120ff
Koster, Helmut 69
Lamar, J.S. 67
laws of thought (see contradiction, excluded middle, identity, rationality, sufficient reason)
limitations
       of thesis 7, 14, 38
logic 50-53
       definition of 27
logical contradiction (see contradiction, logical)
Marle, Rene 65
marriage 41, 46, 48-52, 57, 102
Mickelsen, A. Berkeley 65
objectivity 8
orthotomeo 68
pantheism 19
premises, false 43
presuppositions
       of thesis 7, 14, 36
       proofs of 36
Neilsen, Kai 2

Pinnock, Clark 8, 116
Ramm, Bernard 25
rationality, law of 28, 29, 36
redemption 9
repentance
    necessity of 17
revelation
    definition of 21
    general 93
    immediate 112
    mediate 112
    objective 21
    propositional 21, 87, 113, 115, 117, 124
    special 93ff
Roberts, J.W. 66
Robertson, A.T. 141
Ruby, Lionel 27, 28
salvation 8, 10, 30, 54
    thesis and 32, 39, 102ff, 128ff, 150ff, 163-164
Schramm, Wilbur 24
Shelly, Rubel 46-58
subjectivism 24, 83ff
sufficient reason, law of 29
Terry, Milton 25
thesis 7, 8, 9, 14, 15, 24, 39
    agnosticism and 74
    applications of 154
    argumentation against 14, 134ff
    argumentation in defense of 7, 14, 63, 109ff, 123ff
    epistemology and 29, 38
    hermeneutics and 40
    objections to 7, 14
    practical application of 7, 14
    salvation and 32, 39, 128ff, 150ff, 163-164
Thomas, J.D. 21, 114
Thompson, Samuel M. 99
transposition 78
Trueblood, D. Elton 139
truth 44

      definitional 76
Verderber, Rudolph 24
Warren, Thomas B. 1, 15, 27, 92, 110, 119, 127
Wood, Ledger 29